The Karate Spirit

By
Randall G. Hassell

EMPIRE Books

P.O. Box 491788, Los Angeles, CA 90049

Disclaimer
Please note that the author and publisher of this book are NOT RESPONSIBLE in any manner whatsoever for any injury that may result from practicing the techniques and/or following the instructions given within. Since the physical activities described herein may be too strenuous in nature for some readers to engage in safely, it is essential that a physician be consulted prior to training.

Published in 2006 by Empire Books.

Copyright © 2006 by Randall G. Hassell

Library of Congress Number: 2006010642

ISBN-10: 1-933901-13-6
ISBN-13: 978-1-933901-13-8

Library of Congress Cataloging-in-Publication Data

Hassell, Randall G.
Karate spirit / by Randall G. Hassell. -- 1st ed.
p. cm.
Previously published: St. Louis : Focus Publications, c1995.
Includes index.
ISBN 1-933901-13-6 (pbk. : alk. paper)
1. Karate. I. Title.
GV1114.3.H398 2006
796.815'3--dc22
2006010642

Empire Books LLC
P.O. Box 491788
Los Angeles, CA 90049
(818) 767-9000

06 05 04 03 02 01 00 99 98 97 1 3 5 7 9 10 8 6 4 2
Printed in the United States of America

Table of Contents

Foreword

More than 20 years ago, I set out to write a book on the history of Shotokan karate-do, and I kept getting sidetracked. About every 10 pages or so, I would find myself referring to concepts that had little, if any, written reference in the English language. So, I started listing them and writing columns about them. The columns generated (and continue to generate) mail from around the world.

Some of the letters I receive (like one from an English professor lauding my style) are highly gratifying. Some (like the one from New York that began, "If you ever show your face on the streets in this town, you won't last 20 minutes. We're waiting for you...") are less than gratifying, and some, ("Dear Randall G. Hassell, How does it feel to be a karate spirit?") are simply mystifying.

I truly appreciate all the letters I receive, because they challenge me and make me think.

Lately, I have received many requests for a book collecting "The Karate Spirit" columns. So, for all those who wanted more, I offer this book. For those who never wanted more, rest assured that I have no intention of walking the streets of New York. And for all the rest of you, it feels just fine being a "karate spirit." A little mysterious, perhaps, but just fine.

Randall G. Hassell
St. Louis, Missouri

About the Author

Martial Arts Illustrated magazine called Randall G. Hassell "Shotokan's Great Communicator" and "The spiritual voice for a generation of karate-do practitioners." *The Fighter International* magazine said Hassell is, "hands down, the world's finest, most authoritative karate-do writer."

Chief Instructor of the American Shotokan Karate Alliance (ASKA), President of the American JKA Karate Association International (AJKA-I), and Senior Editor of Tamashii Press, Randall Hassell is a professional writer and editor who began karate training in 1960. He also is a first generation American to pioneer Shotokan karate, introducing it to the St. Louis, Missouri area in 1961.

While majoring in English Literature at Washington University in St. Louis, he began an intense, formal study of the history and philosophy of the martial arts in general, and karate-do in particular.

To date, this study has led to the publication of more than 100 articles in numerous periodicals around the world, and more than 28 books including:

The Complete Idiot's Guide to Karate; Recognition: A Karate Novel (with Stan Schmidt); *The Karate Experience: A Way of Life; Conversations with the Master: Masatoshi Nakayama; Shotokan Karate: Its History and Evolution; Karate Ideals; The Karate Spirit; Karate Training Guide Volume 1: Foundations of Training; Karate Training Guide Volume 2: Kata—Heian, Tekki, Bassai Dai; Samurai Journey* (with Osamu Ozawa).

In addition to teaching in his own *dojo* and at various YMCAs and school districts in the St. Louis, Missouri metro area, Mr. Hassell oversees the instruction and administration of thousands of students nationwide in ASKA and AJKA affiliated clubs, and he travels extensively, teaching, lecturing, and officiating.

TALKING ABOUT KARATE

I have always loved to talk. According to my mother, I started talking at a very rapid rate when I was six months old, and my mouth has been active ever since. It is a pleasurable habit that has served me well in times of need, such as in school when I had not the faintest idea what the teacher was talking about. When called upon, I would scan the book in front of me, summon my best facial expressions, and pour out phrases laced with key words from the material at hand. Most of the time this system worked, undoubtedly more from the teacher tiring of listening to me than from the accuracy of what I had to say. Nevertheless, it served to convince me at an early age of the efficacy of words.

Words are a powerful weapon in clever hands, and I have been enamored of their use for as long as I can remember. Not only have they saved me from punishment for laziness in studying, but on numerous occasions they have saved my body from abuse at the hands of the neighborhood bully. As a small-ish, bespectacled child, I was a natural target for those among my peers whose best mental efforts were located in their fists. When threatened, I would launch a verbal counterattack, calling into question the relationship of the attacker's actions to the great men of peace—Ghandi, Schweitzer and, not least, Jerry. Jerry was five years older than me, and a Golden Gloves boxing champion who "let" me help him with his homework. I was good at this, and retired undefeated into my teens without a single split lip or black eye.

Then came karate.

At the age of 12, Japanese karate-do moved into first place in my life, and in the ensuing almost twenty-five years, it has given me the things I missed as a child. I have had split lips, black eyes, a bloody nose (as I recall, my nose bled continuously between my junior and senior years in high school), some broken toes, a couple of jammed fingers, and enough bruises to make my family doctor the world's leading authority on hematoma. But most important of all, karate taught me the difference between just talking and really having something to say.

By the time I was a seventeen-year-old brown belt, I still thought my words were clever, intelligent and useful. That is probably what I was thinking when my instructor caught me lecturing a new student in the dressing room. He listened for a few minutes and then said, "Enough talk. Let's go."

Throughout the class that followed, I continued to talk to the beginner, correcting his stance, explaining the meaning of his training, and so on. Near the end of the hour, my instructor called me up to the front of the class and asked me in a loud voice, "Mr. Hassell, do you like girls?"

"Uh, well, yes, Sensei, I do."

"Do you have a girlfriend?"

"A girlfriend?" I asked, thoroughly bewildered.

"Yes, Mr. Hassell. I'm speaking English. A girlfriend. "

"Yes, Sensei, I have a girlfriend."

"Do you ever arm wrestle with her?" he shouted.

"No, Sensei! I never arm wrestle with my girlfriend!"

7

"Good!" he shouted. "You are so weak, she would beat you! You are the most terriblest brown belt I ever see! All talk! No action!"

"Thank you, Sensei!" I replied crisply.

"You are welcome," he replied. "Get back in line."

A lot of years have passed since that day of the great embarrassment, but I have never forgotten the lesson I learned. Now that I am older and supposedly wiser, I have carefully begun talking again. This was necessary to provide my own students with the lessons I learned the hard way. I want them to learn the easy way, if possible. But I have to be careful. If I talk too much and listen too little, I will face another day of embarrassment at the hands of my instructor or my seniors. This is the way of karate-do.

For more than two decades, I have spent the bulk of my time practicing karate-do, the way of life of the empty hand. That is what I will talk about in this monthly column, and I hope readers who practice other arts will not think that I am ignoring them. I simply talk and write about what I know best. So if you can bear up a bit, I will talk to anyone who cares to listen, for as long as I can think of something to say. I will try

to provide something with human interest, something that has a touch of humor and/or irony, and something that stimulates your thought processes. Some of my writings will end like a *koan*, leaving the reader dangling on the horns of his own interpretation.

There is one thing I should confess. I teach karate to several hundred students, but I don't operate a commercial school, and this sometimes puts me in unwanted conflict with others in my area who do run commercial schools and make their living at it. Recently, one of my students happened to meet one of the local instructors whose school is near my *dojo*. The instructor was accompanied by a young man who had come to our *dojo*, watched a few classes, and decided to enroll elsewhere.

"Oh, Hassell," said the instructor. "You don't want to train with him! He thinks karate is some sort of way of life or something, that takes forever. You ought to join our school. We don't mess around with all that spirit stuff; we just teach you to fight. If you train with me, you'll be able to whip anybody around inside of six months."

"Yeah," echoed his student. "I watched Hassell doing his thing, and he wants you to practice all the time. I think he's got an attitude problem."

To both of these accusations I plead guilty in the first degree. If believing in the intrinsic values of karate-do for human beings and insisting that students train hard every day are beliefs worthy of punishment, then I am surely going to spend eternity in a super-heated condition.

"PUREES PRAHKTEES KARATES"

Looking back over more than twenty years of karate training, almost all of it under Japanese instructors, I have to believe that the greatest barrier faced by students and teachers alike is that of language.

The first Japanese karate instructors started arriving in the United States around 1960, and while they possessed extraordinary skills in karate, they possessed almost no skill in English communications. This was a source of great frustration for both students and teachers.

My earliest recollections of training flash through my mind in Japanese. I couldn't understand Japanese, of course, but that was less a problem than it might appear at first glance. What the instructors could not say, they demonstrated. And we were left to imitate their movements over and over and over again. When we were at a complete loss in grasping what we were being told verbally, the instructors always managed to get through to us on a most basic level. I recall, for instance, a class under a famed Japanese master who at that time spoke almost no English, but always managed to communicate. One time we were all standing in line, waiting to practice our basic techniques.

"Reftu regu furontu, kokutsu-dachi," he commanded.

We were white belts with only a couple of months of training under our belts, but most of us understood what he meant. We all snapped our left legs forward in *kokutsu-dachi*, the back stance. And we had little trouble getting the idea to return to our starting position each time, alternating legs and executing knife-hand blocks. As the instructor walked down the line, he would correct the form of each student, always speaking Japanese, which we did not understand, but also physically positioning our bodies, which we understood clearly.

When he got to me, he moved my arms a bit, kicked my front leg into position, and then stood directly in front of me with his hands on his hips.

"Huh-uh," he said, and then proceeded to speak to me rapidly in Japanese, assuming a stance in front of me and pointing to various points on his body.

"Unnastan?" he asked.

"*Hai*!" I assured him, having absolutely no idea what he was talking about.

Then, still talking, he raised his back leg high into the air, and in slow motion, brought it around in a wide arc, executing a classical roundhouse kick. The ball of his foot came down directly on the top of my head, and he rested his foot there, still talking.

"Unnastan?" he asked again, after a minute or two.

"Yes, Sensei!" I shouted.

"Very good!" he said, slowly lowering his leg along the same path from which it had come.

To this day, I have not the slightest idea of what he said to me, but whenever I practice knife-hand blocks in back stance, I still remember the awe I felt at seeing that man perform such an incredible kick. And I also adjust my arms and legs properly and tense my buttocks.

By the mid-1960s, of course, the Japanese had learned to speak more English, and most of us had learned to understand a little Japanese, but sometimes our individual efforts to communicate in foreign tongues caused more trouble than the efforts were worth.

In 1970, I was directing a large tournament, and most of the judges were Japanese instructors who had been in the United States for several years. The night before the tournament, I had a conversation with the Chief Judge about the curiosities of speaking a foreign language. While he was talking, I noticed that when he was speaking English, he always added an "s" to the end of karate, pronouncing it "karates." Some of these things occurred, he said, because he was thinking in English and, therefore, was giving the English pronunciation of Japanese words. When he "thought" in Japanese, the words came out differently.

At the tournament the next day, I learned first-hand how silly I must sound to my Japanese teachers when I tried to think in Japanese, and also how incredibly difficult it must be for them to think in English.

Between two of the events, the Chief Judge rushed over to the table where I was sitting and said, "Now changing plan, please."

"Okay, Sensei," I said. "What shall we change?"

"Now try quahm," he said distinctly.

"Quahm?" I asked.

"No, no," he responded. "Quahm."

"I'm sorry, Sensei. I don't know what you mean. What's quahm?"

He seemed a bit frustrated. "Quahm!" he said more forcefully. "You know, quahm division."

"*Wakarimasen*," I said in Japanese. "I don't understand. I'm sorry."

"Okay, okay," he said. "I writing. Your pen, please."

I handed him my pen, and he wrote F-O-R-M. "There," he said. "Quahm."

"Form?" I asked incredulously.

"Yes!" he cried happily.

"Oh, form!" I repeated. "You mean form like in *kata*—formal exercise."

"Yes," he said. "*Kata!*"

I wondered at the time why in the name of sanity he didn't just say *kata* and be done with it. But now I realize that the Chief Judge must have felt a bit like Mark Twain, who said, "In Paris, they simply stared when I spoke to them in French; I never did succeed in making those idiots understand their own language."

SAKKI

O ne of the things all serious martial artists aspire to attain is the ability to sense *sakki*, which literally means "air of murder." *Sakki* is the word the Japanese use to describe the feeling, or vibration, that comes from an attacker just before he is about to attack. It is said that if one can learn to sense this feeling, a counterattack can be applied before the actual attack occurs.

In Japan, people will even say that certain swords or works of art emanate this mysterious force, and it is very common to hear references to swords which have an air of murder, a la King Arthur's famous blade, which he plucked from the rock.

In the West, almost everyone has sensed a *sakki* at one time or another. It is the vague feeling of uneasiness that permeates the mind and body for no particular reason when we walk into a room full of unfamiliar people. Sometimes we just get the feeling that "something's not right here."

Mothers are renowned for their uncanny sense of *sakki*, which manifests itself in them in late night calls to children far away. "I just had an uneasy feeling about you," they say. Mothers call this intuition.

But no matter what it is called, the ability to sense *sakki* is a high ideal of the martial arts, and if a person could actually develop the ability to sense things in this manner, he or she would be taking a giant step toward invulnerability.

After more than two decades of training, I have come to believe that it is possible to develop this sense, but I also think it takes a lot longer for some than a mere couple of decades to get the gist of it.

In the Japan Karate Association, one tale of *sakki* is told by virtually every master to virtually ever black belt holder, and while the story is ascribed to Masatomo Takagi, the Vice Chairman of the JKA, all Takagi will do when questioned about it is smile, nod, and say, "Yes, that's true. It happened to all of us."

The story goes that before World War II, when Gichin Funakoshi was traveling around Japan giving demonstrations to promote karate, he would take along a senior student or two to assist him. It was the duty of this assistant to help the instructor with the demonstrations and to tend to his personal needs. When they visited a university club, Funakoshi would sit on the side in a state of deep concentration and direct the actions of the assistant who was teaching the class.

Funakoshi one day told his senior assistants that it was difficult for him to train consistently because he was traveling so much. Therefore, he said, the seniors should help him train so that he, too, could progress in his art.

"The way you can help me," he told them, "is at any time, under any conditions, simply punch me or kick me. If you can hit me, it will mean that I'm not aware enough and that I must train harder."

The seniors had no intention of doing such a thing, of course, because they loved the old man, and they were afraid they might hurt him. But as time went by and no one attacked him, Funakoshi became irritable. "I told you to help me train, and you have disobeyed. I want you to try to punch me and kick me. It is the only way I can progress."

So the seniors decided they would abide by his wishes, but would use control so he would not be injured.

One day as Masatomo Takagi was teaching a class, he noticed that Funakoshi, who was sitting on the edge of the training floor, had dozed off and was snoring gently.

"Now's my chance," Takagi thought. "I'll punch his face lightly, and he will see that this is a silly thing for us to be doing."

Continuing to talk to the class in his normal tone of voice, Takagi gradually positioned himself within striking distance of the snoring Funakoshi. When he was convinced that the teacher's snores were rhythmical and genuine, he suddenly snapped around and drove a blindingly fast punch at the old man's head.

Without opening his eyes, Funakoshi leaned his head to the right, deftly avoiding the punch with at least three inches of space to spare. Opening his eyes, he looked at the startled senior and said, simply, "Not good enough, Takagi. You need to train more." So saying, he closed his eyes and was soon snoring again.

As Takagi told and re-told this story to the other seniors, he was scoffed at and teased. "Sensei was tricking you," they said. "He wasn't really sleeping. He was just playing cat and mouse with you. Nobody can defend himself when he's asleep. Try it again when there is no chance that he's awake, and then we can be done with this nonsense."

Takagi's chance came not long after, while he was accompanying Funakoshi on a demonstration tour. After a demonstration and lecture in a village in the country, Funakoshi retired to his rented room, and Takagi took the instructor's clothes to wash them. When he returned, he peered into Funakoshi's room and saw that he was lying on his back, snoring, with his arm across his eyes.

"This is perfect," Takagi thought. "Even if he's awake, he can't see through his arm. I'll get him for sure this time."

When Takagi entered the room and laid out Funakoshi's clothes, the old man didn't stir. So Takagi crept stealthily toward the old man and stopped about four feet away. Sensing no movement in Funakoshi, Takagi began thinking that this really had gone too far. He didn't want to hit the defenseless old man, and besides, he decided, he could simply tell his teacher in the morning that he had stood beside him, punched close to his face, and that would be that.

While Takagi stood there clenching his fists and thinking about it, Funakoshi suddenly said in a clear, loud voice, "Takagi, if you're going to punch me, please do it and get it over with! I'm an old man, and I need my sleep!"

It is said that Masatomo Takagi, then fifth degree black belt, backed out of Funakoshi's room at great speed and never again tried to attack his teacher.

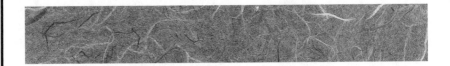

A NON-PROFIT DOJO
(BUT WE DIDN'T PLAN IT THAT WAY)

During an interview with Masatoshi Nakayama, headmaster of the Japan Karate Association, I tried my best, in the staid tradition of Western journalism, to get him to say something controversial. Something that would raise a few hackles and sell a few magazines. If only he would say something like those folks say in the *National Enquirer*, we would have our famous cover: "KARATE GRANDMASTER SAYS FULL-CONTACT JOKE." But Nakayama disappointed me. He didn't criticize anybody or anything. (For the record, he said that full-contact karate is fine for people who want to do it, and that it certainly has a place in the world of karate, just so long as everyone understands that it is a sport and not *budo*. And he also said, ending my dreams of fame and notoriety, "...and there's certainly nothing wrong with making contact.") So much for trying to trick the master.

Over the course of several days of interviewing, only once did I see Nakayama shake his head in disgust and shoot a little bit of fire out of his eyes. We were talking about the history and development of karate in America, and during a lull in the conversation, he leaned over, close to my face, gritted his teeth, and said, very sternly, "You know what's really wrong with our karate?" he asked.

Our karate? I thought. Isn't it the other guys who are screwed up?

"What's really wrong with our karate," he continued, "is that people train a few years, make first or second *dan*, and then right away open a school and try to make money from karate. They're not qualified to teach by themselves and, besides, it's impossible to make money quickly from true karate-do."

He didn't have to convince me on the money factor. Over the years, I have seen many, many instructors open commercial schools and then make the mistake of teaching their students true karate-do, in the traditional fashion. Invariably, these people quickly learn that the traditional ways are not, by and large, easily marketable. Oh, it's easy enough to attract a fair-sized student body—with skillful advertising and promotion—but boy-oh-boy, is it ever hard to keep them! The main problem, as I see it, is that we are offering our customers something they don't really want.

Gichin Funakoshi warned us of the problem in one of his famous "Twenty Precepts." He said, *"Karate no shugyo wa issho de aru,"* which means, "Karate practice is lifetime work; there is no limit." An equally accurate translation is, "it will take your entire life to learn karate."

For those of us who try to follow Funakoshi's precepts, the road to mastery is long, arduous and fraught with disappointments. What we are saying to the prospective student, really, is, "Join our *dojo*, pay your money, and we will push you, humiliate you, discipline you, and make you work harder than you have ever worked in your life. If you continue training, we will demand that you pay more money for harder and harder work, stricter discipline, and continuing self-sacrifice."

Clearly, we place ourselves in the middle of a harsh, inflexible paradox: We are marketing karate-do, but karate-do has little to commend it to the American market.

A colleague of mine says that we are asking people to enroll in school for their own betterment and then shocking them with the news that there is no graduation day. He's right.

There are a number of traditionalists around, of course, who are supremely successful, and they have hundreds, even thousands, of students. But not one of them was an overnight

19

success. Each one of them, to the best of my knowledge, had to work long and hard, enduring many hardships and setbacks, to "make it" in the business world. Every one of them that I know had to endure terrible frustrations and poverty on the way to business success.

Frankly, in the spirit of karate-do, this is the way it should be, because the benefits derived from serious pursuit of the ideals of karate-do are too valuable to be priced and sold. How much should be charged, for example, for good health, good appetite, good digestion, blissful sleep or boundless energy? How much is it worth to have confidence, self-assurance and mental clarity? Can a price really be placed on being happy with yourself and happy with others, no matter how they act? Probably not, but these things are clearly by-products of hard, daily training under a good instructor.

And, yes, we traditionalists really believe that correct training will bring all these assets to the serious student. But the problem remains, as my friend so aptly put it, that we cannot tell the student when graduation day will be, because we know it will never come. As long as the student keeps training, he will improve—continuously until the day he dies.

One karate instructor, Shojiro Koyama of Phoenix, Arizona, was showing us some of the physical benefits of daily training last year, and he inadvertently hinted at how long it might take to get to "graduation day." Facing the wall, about one foot away from it, Koyama spread his legs straight to the sides, heels and toes touching the floor, and performed a complete split, his crotch touching the floor. He then invited two husky black belts to grasp his ankles and lift him into the air. "Just lift straight up," he said, and he kept his hands on the wall for balance as they hoisted him high above their heads, his crotch now a bit lower than his legs. When they put him down, he sprang to his feet, turned to us and said, "I am 46 years old, but karate-do has made me able to do this kind of thing. You can do it, too. Don't say no; just practice a little bit every day, and after ten years, you will be able to do it, too. Every step of karate-do takes at least ten years, but when you get to be my age, you will realize that it's worth the effort."

Worth the effort, but not easily marketable.

Of course, the bright side to all of this is that traditional karate-do offers a solid philosophy based on physical education, sport and self-defense, and more and more people in our society are being attracted to all three. The here-today-gone-tomorrow studios of the Bruce Lee© era are not much in evidence now, and the public is discovering that the old, plain, run-down place on the corner, that was there before the modern studios moved in and out, is still there. It still has the same instructor, and he appears to be doing the same old things. His students in their white uniforms are still doing the same things they were ten years ago, and even though they look stern and serious and sweaty, they genuinely seem to be enjoying what they are doing.

As public interest in traditional karate-do continues to grow, and as enrollment in the traditional *dojo* increases, I hope instructors and students alike will meditate on the words of the ancient sage, Mencius, who said:

When Heaven is about to confer
A great office upon a man,
It first exercises his mind with suffering,
His sinews and bones with toil.
It exposes him to poverty,
And confounds all his undertakings.
Then it is seen if he is ready.

Or, as Master Funakoshi warned, "It will take your entire life to learn karate."

FINDING *MYO*

Technology has been helpful to modern karate. It used to be that a stop by the *dojo* where I trained on Sunday afternoon found people banging away on the *makiwara* or doing *kata* or free-sparring. When I stop by my own *dojo* these days, several students are usually there doing those things, but more often than not, they are doing them in front of a video camera. Over and over they perform their *kata*, and then they sit down to watch it in instant replay on a portable television.

The videotape recorder is a wonderful invention. It enables us to practice and then view our practice immediately afterwards. Theoretically, this helps us see our own flaws, which, with the slightest of effort, can then be corrected. The video camera thus is thought to improve performance.

Unfortunately, the video camera doesn't significantly improve our karate-do, because it doesn't help us find *myo*.

Myo is the state of mind and being which we all should be striving for in karate-do. It is a creative and original force emanating from the unconscious, or from the "original mind." Myo is the state of mind of the true master, who moves creatively and spontaneously from his unconscious, irrespective of technique or skill or universal concepts of how things ought to look. It is the state of the spider spinning its web, the bee building its hive, the cool breeze blowing softly across the dew at dawn.

Myo is attained when the conscious mind delves deeply into the unconscious and transcends rationality and intellection. Only in a state of *myo*, it is said, can the true nature of things be realized, and the lines between physical, psychological and metaphysical reality be destroyed. Only in a state of *myo* can spiritual mastery be attained, and then only because the student has transcended even the desire to attain it. To desire is to choose, and to choose is to make an intellectual decision. But mastery lies beyond this level.

Needless to say, attainment of *myo* is a lofty and worthy goal, but it will not be reached with electronic machines, no matter how flawlessly they measure every physical aspect of performance. The main problem with machines is that they cause us to think, and thinking is bad for karate development. Doing is the only thing that helps us find *myo*, and the more we think, the less we do.

I know this is true, because I listen to the students when they are watching tapes of themselves. "See that?" they cry, "My

back foot is turned out! Oh, no! I'm not moving my arms at the same time! My rear end's sticking out!" And on and on.

The camera now routinely makes its way to tournaments and demonstrations, of course, and when tapes of these events are viewed, I hear comments like, "Oh, oh. Master so-and-so isn't doing that right. His leg is bent. And look at that! His whole body bounced when he did that one!" This is always followed by, "Yeah, he's not doing it right, but you tell him."

While all this is fun and obviously helps students refine some details of their technique, I wish I could explain to them how useless it is. I haven't found *myo* myself, but as in every other aspect of my development, I am seeking it by following the advice of Gichin Funakoshi. He left us in his "Twenty Precepts," the way to find *myo*. Funakoshi said, *"Arai-yuru mono wo karate-ka seyo, soko ni myo-mi, ari,"* which means, "Put your everyday living into karate and you will find *myo*, or, as one master simplified it for me, "Karate-ize everything."

What this implies is that there should be no demarcations between karate training and the business of day-do-day life. It implies that we should break our psychological attachments to "things" and especially to thinking and theorizing. In karate this is manifested in the strong emphasis placed on allowing the body to move freely through intuition. Thinking takes time, and time creates a pause in movement. A pause in *kata* appears as a jerky, unnatural movement. In sparring it appears as instant defeat. In everyday living, too much thinking about the potential consequences of a decision results in frustration and anxiety. Facing a difficult life decision should be viewed in the same light as facing a skilled opponent: let your mind mirror your opponent (problem), and strike forcefully from the center of your being the instant you sense an opening.

By breaking our attachments to illusions through karate-do, we eliminate doubt and suspicion. This is basic to the idea of *budo*, which means "to stop conflict." In the *dojo*, the elimination of doubt and suspicion is supported by the demand for complete trust and faith in the wisdom and experience of the instructor. When we are suspicious of the motives or intentions of friends or business acquaintances, it is frequently because we have not eliminated the conflicts in our own thinking. Through trusting our partners in sparring, we learn that self-respect is the foundation of respect for others.

The calm mind strived for in karate-do is developed in training by learning to withhold one's inner feelings from the opponent. The stable emotions gained in sparring and self-defense can then serve the student in any stressful situation. Through training we can learn how to control our emotions and overcome anxiety. When we can overcome anxiety even faced with direct attack, we will find day-to-day stresses far less problematic.

An important principle along the path of finding *myo* is that what we see on the outside is a reflection of what is inside us. That is, fear of an opponent, for example, does not lie in the opponent, but only inside the one who is afraid. Thus, gain control over yourself, and you will gain control over the opponent. In this regard we may say that actions are the mirror of the mind. What a person does reveals more about him than what he says. At the same time, the mind is the mirror of actions. That is, those who are truly modest and sincere in their minds will act modest and sincere in their daily lives. Those who feel inferior will work the hardest to impress others.

From these basic connections, each student can begin to live by the precepts of his art, both in the *dojo* and out, and can start finding *myo*.

So, you ask, what's wrong with videotaping a kata and then reviewing the tape to help improve my karate?

There's nothing wrong with it at all except: a) it takes time away from you which could better be spent practicing and trying to break through to the essence of yourself as a human being; b) it gives you the false impression that precision of technique is the most important facet of karate training, when in fact the development of each individual as a human being is the most important facet; c) it makes you think about the details of physical techniques instead of feeling the essence of those techniques through practice; d) it makes you look at how a master performs his techniques rather than at why he performs them; e) it makes you think that karate is some special, separate part of your life which can be analyzed, dissected and ultimately mastered through close scrutiny, when in fact it is more like brushing your teeth; f) a videotape cannot accurately record feeling, emotion or sense of being; and g) it doesn't help you "karate-ize" anything or help you find *myo*.

Other than that, there's nothing wrong with it. Nothing at all.

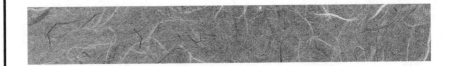

CONTROL

I recently came upon the second-best definition of *kime* (focus) I have ever heard: "*Kime* is not the development of power; it is the application, coordination and concentration of it." Actually, if definitions are measured in words only, this is the very best definition I have ever heard. But sometimes, particularly in *budo*, definitions are more accurately perceived in another sense.

Ron Johnson of the East Coast Karate Association reminded me of the best definition of *kime* I have yet come across. A student of JKA master Teruyuki Okazaki since the early 1960s, Johnson recalled how Okazaki defined *kime* for his students back then.

"We were all training and trying our best to understand *kime*, but Sensei just wasn't satisfied with our performance," Johnson said. "He kept saying that we were hitting too hard and showing no control of our power.

"The harder we tried to understand and do it right, the farther away we got from what we were supposed to be doing. Finally, in exasperation, Sensei got some toilet tissue from the bathroom and he had a student hold three connected sheets in front of him. 'This,' he said, 'is what you are doing.' With that, he punched the strip of tissue and tore it in half. Directing the student to hold up another strip of three sheets, he said, 'This is *kime*.' He punched again, but this time a hole appeared only in the center tissue, and the other two sheets were left intact. The fragile perforations were not broken; there was just that unbelievable hole in the center!"

The operative word here is control. The strongest man in the world could not duplicate Okazaki's feat without the arduous training needed to apply, coordinate and concentrate his power. It was not Okazaki's awesome power that enabled him to punch a hole in the tissue; it was his awesome control of his power.

I was thinking about this the other day while thumbing through the karate ads in the new Yellow Pages to see what was up. I noted that the larger the ad, the more benefits it listed as by-products of karate training. Different schools claim different benefits, but every one of them offered the two benefits of "confidence" and "self-control."

In my *dojo* we have five guidelines enshrined on the front wall—the five guidelines left to us by Gichin Funakoshi. One of them, loosely translated, is "to control bad temper," and I decided to question some of my own students about that principle.

"What does that mean," I asked, "to control bad temper?" The answers were, I think, typical of karate people everywhere:

"It means don't get mad."

"It means don't lose your temper."

"It means to always be calm and never get angry."

Reasonable responses all, but they all miss the heart of the matter. "To control bad temper" doesn't mean that you should not get mad, nor does it mean that you should not have a bad temper. We are human beings after all, and we all have a bad temper from time to time.

In the context of *budo*, "to control bad temper," in fact means that you should have a bad temper now and again, that you should bring it out, study it, confront it, and use it to your best advantage. One should, again by the "second best" definition, apply it, coordinate it and concentrate it.

Oh, no, you say. The purpose of *budo* is to make people calm and help them transcend fear, temper and all the other destructive human emotions.

Nonsense, I say. The purpose of *budo* training is certainly to make people calm, but this does not mean that they should be

29

stripped of their basic human emotions. Indeed, in the traditional martial ways the purpose of *budo* training is to make people confront themselves, to become aware of their emotions and feelings—both good and bad, positive and negative—and to learn to control them. Without confronting and experiencing emotions like anger, hatred, love and so on, it is utterly impossible for people to have a calm, controlled mind.

Masatoshi Nakayama, Chief Instructor of the Japan Karate Association, told me that control of techniques is gained by developing those techniques to their most powerful levels and then controlling them at whatever level is necessary at the moment. According to Nakayama, the best way to do this is to practice rigorously on the *makiwara* (padded striking post). Let the power come out, he says, so you can see it and feel it. Then you will have a chance to recognize it and control it.

This is sound advice for learning to control techniques and, I think, equally sound for learning to control emotions.

In Greek tragedy the process of the hero confronting all his bad emotions and feelings and breaking through them to a state of calm is called catharsis, and the traditional ways of *budo* have their own form of catharsis. Essentially, the *budo* system revolves around the idea of the instructor pushing his students to their limits, putting them under stress in the controlled atmosphere of the *dojo* and making them cope. The most stressful situation available to human beings is physical attack with the threat of injury or death. Our strongest biological responses are geared to respond to this kind of stress. It is important that we deal with those responses in a controlled environment so we will recognize them if we are actually attacked. In other words, it is necessary for us to experience fear and confusion and temper in the *dojo* so we can deal with them and learn to control them before we go outside and confront a mugger.

Another facet of the instructor's responsibility is to act in the fashion of the Zen master who said, "I have nothing to reveal to you by words. If I did you might later have cause to hold me up to ridicule. My job is to give you thirty raps on the head whether you affirm or negate. Do not speak out and do not remain silent. This is the only way you will understand."

Accordingly, not only must the student be put in situations that elicit strong emotional responses, but must also be forced to work through those responses by himself. He must learn to control his emotions but not eliminate them.

During a clinic, a teacher asked one day, "Are there any questions? Several hands went up along with mine, and he patiently answered all the questions except mine.

"You are too stupid to understand the answer," he said.

Later in the same month he asked me to attend a meeting of advanced students and instructors during which, after he outlined a complicated plan about an administrative matter, he again asked, "Are there any questions?" But I had learned my lesson well and silently stared at the table in front of me.

"Mr. Hassell," he said, "don't you have any questions?"

"No, Sensei," I replied, "none at all."

"You are stupid!" he shouted. "You are willing to just sit there like a lamb going to slaughter and let me lead you down the path! Use your brain for a change!"

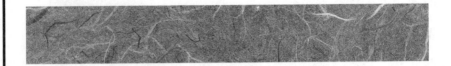

SEEING AND KNOWING

In traditional Japanese karate tournaments, team *kata* is one of the most demanding, difficult events. Three contestants perform the same *kata* as a team, and they are judged on how closely together they perform the movements. The more they look and sound like one person, the higher the score. Even more important and difficult is that they must all understand the *kata* and project the important elements of individual *kata* performance: intensity, timing, balance, understanding of movements, projection of feeling, correct application of power, expansion and contraction of the body, correct application of speed and slowness, and so on. Even the slightest error on the part of one of the contestants results in a drastic reduction of points from the judges.

One of the finest examples of team *kata* I ever witnessed was at a Japanese-style national championship in the late 1970s. The competition was fierce. Contestants were atypically choosing to do very complicated, advanced *kata* in the team event, which is usually bereft of any sort of *kata* except the most basic, evenly timed ones. But on this day, a team came out and performed Unsu, an extraordinarily difficult *kata* which features drastic changes in timing from slow to fast, radical changes in direction of movement and a 360-degree turn in mid-air. Nothing could top that performance, we thought. But much to our delight, the fourth team to appear announced that their team *kata* would be Nijushiho, a *kata* with even more difficult timing than Unsu.

As we watched the performance, we held our breath as it became apparent that this team was performing flawlessly.

Every nuance of movement was performed as if one person was temporarily divided into three. Their performance was magnificent, and when the scores were announced and it was apparent that they had tied for first place with the Unsu team, the auditorium erupted in prolonged applause.

The only thing more difficult than doing team *kata* in high-level competition is doing a tie-breaker team *kata* in high-level

competition. In preparing for team competition, teams naturally choose one *kata* and practice it together hour after hour, day after day, month after month. Accordingly, they tend to neglect other *kata* in hopes of achieving the one outstanding performance that will trounce their opponents. Tie-breaking *kata* thus becomes a serious problem for the team. They have rarely practiced a second *kata* together, yet the tie-breaker is

judged even more rigorously than the first *kata*; the judges are looking carefully for even the slightest variance in movement because no one wants another tie.

On this day the Unsu team opted for Bassai Dai for their tie-breaker. Bassai Dai is a powerful, dynamic *kata* with relatively basic timing. The Nijushiho team, however, chose Tekki Nidan, another complicated *kata* requiring extremely close coordination and highly varied timing. We later learned that neither team had really practiced a second *kata* in preparation for the tournament, so the selection of Tekki Nidan was a bold move on the part of the Nijushiho team. By selecting it they were in fact expressing confidence in their team captain. He would be in front of the other two team members, and his timing would have to be flawless so they could follow it.

When they came out on the floor, it seemed odd that the two other team members appeared to be escorting the team captain to the center of the contest area. Indeed, they each held one of his arms, walked with him to the center mark, and then moved back to their contest positions.

Much to everyone's surprise and delight, they performed their *kata* as if they had invented it. There was no hesitation as they moved from the slow, opening movements to the staccato stepping and blocking movements and then back to slow. Their performance was flawless, and the intensity of feeling coming out of their eyes was stunning. As they returned to the natural stance after completing the *kata* with a sharp *kiai*, the crowd hesitated a moment and then broke into wild applause. There was no question in the minds of the spectators which team had come out on top in the tie-breaker. This second team had devastated their competition.

After the applause died down following the announcement of the Nijushiho/Tekki Nidan team's victory, the announcer did something rarely done at Japanese-style karate tournaments. Speaking gently and smoothly he said, "Ladies and gentlemen, we rarely comment on the performance of individuals at these tournaments because the purpose of karate-do is not winning or losing, nor does it revolve around who is the best athlete. We are here to test each other and see how our techniques are progressing in their development. Today, however, we have witnessed a truly remarkable display of timing, agility and grace under pressure, and we feel that it deserves special recognition. The champion team in this competition performed two of the most difficult *kata* in karate—Nijushiho and Tekki Nidan. These *kata* are not generally used in team competition because

of their difficult timing and complex movements. What you saw were three athletes performing as one. They have worked hard and long to perfect their *kata,* and even though they had not practiced the second *kata* together very much as a team, they have practiced so intensely individually that they were able to give us this extraordinary performance.

"Even though we don't usually point out extraordinary achievements in the karate arena, both the Chief Judge and I feel that all of you should know that this particular performance is truly an exception. It is the proof of our contention that doing karate is the most important thing, and that just going through the movements has little value.

"Ladies and gentlemen, the team captain of the winning team is completely blind."

Contrary to what you may be expecting, this story is not about the marvel of a handicapped person making it big in the martial arts. It is a story about how to learn karate. A Chinese proverb illuminates the essence of learning for us:

To see is to understand.

To do is to know.

Whether one has 20/20 vision or is completely blind, the process of knowing karate is the same: to do is to know. The blind team captain deserves no accolades simply because he has mastered a difficult physical art without sight. He deserves accolades because he has done karate more than the rest of us. He is living proof of the maxim I heard repeated so often by my instructor, especially when I would look around at my seniors during class to see how they were performing a particular technique. The instructor would whack me on the rump or sweep me to the floor, always with the same admonition: "Don't think; just do!"

Now I understand what he meant.

KARATE AND HEALTH

The other day, I was reading an article in a martial arts magazine about a very famous American karate champion, now retired from competition, but nevertheless highly regarded as a fine physical specimen. Since he is past 40, he was saying, he has to really be careful about his health and conditioning. He works out with religious fervor, he explained, every Monday, Wednesday and Friday, three hours at a time. He described his training regimen in detail—so many push-ups, so many sit-ups of this type, so many squats of that type, so many front kicks in the air, so many kicks against the heavy bag, and so on.

In addition to his specific physical regimen, he was convinced that the only way to maintain good health was through a diet consisting of lean meats, fish, fruits and vegetables, supplementing this with special protein drinks and vitamins.

As I looked at his deeply lined face in the photos, my mind wandered to a story Shojiro Koyama, Chief Instructor of the Arizona Karate Association in Phoenix, had told me about karate and health. Koyama later printed this episode in the Tournament Program of his 17th Annual Western States Karate Championships. It is a story about Masatoshi Nakayama, Chief Instructor of the Japan Karate Association, and about his two-month visit to the United States, the Caribbean and Mexico. The 69-year-old Nakayama toured and taught continuously during the hottest months of the year in 1982—July and August—and kept a pace that would be very difficult even for a young adult.

According to Koyama, "Normally, such an itinerary would be close to impossible for someone the age of Nakayama. He spent one week in Arizona, including four days in Flagstaff. I spent much of this time with him, and I questioned him about his diet and exercise regimen, understanding, of course, his lifetime devotion to karate and the martial arts.

"His response was, 'I eat everything.' Chinese food, Mexican food, even a Cowboy Steak were among the many types of meals that we had during his stay. He seemed to have a great love of hot salsa on his Mexican food and also enjoyed tenderloin steaks. Much of what we had during that week was very contrary to what dietitians and nutritionists would prescribe as a sensible diet.

"Again I asked him for his secret of good health and long life. He responded with a smile and said, 'Just practice karate every day.' He also related a story from 1935, when he was a sophomore university student and he traveled to China and into the Mongolian desert on his own. The trip was lonely, and at night when the sun went down, he felt as if the surrounding desert was virtually absorbing him. So powerful was this experience that it provided him with a great personal reserve and philosophy for the rest of his life.

"We visited the OK Corral in Tombstone, Arizona one day in mid-July. On the way, he requested that we stop so that he might photograph some scenery. Unfortunately, the temperature was over 115 degrees. I have lived in Arizona for over sixteen years, but after following Nakayama for ten minutes, I developed a headache. I asked the master to please come out of the heat and back to the air conditioned car so we might con-

tinue our trip. His reply was that he really didn't mind the heat, having survived temperatures in the Mongolian desert of close to 130 degrees.

"While he never said so directly, I have made the following observations and drawn conclusions on what Nakayama's

secrets of long life and good health are. First is a one hundred percent commitment to whatever he is doing, whether teaching, sightseeing or eating. Second, physiologically, his brain devotes total concentration and energy to one task at a time, never dividing the energy among several tasks. Third, he does not dwell on what is 'tomorrow,' but more on enjoying all of 'today.' Fourth, his experiences in Manchuria and the Mongolian desert have caused him to become very spiritually independent.

"I sincerely feel that his opinions on lifestyle are much more valuable than what is contained in the pages of any book on diet, nutrition or exercise."

Thinking about Koyama's words, I continued reading the words of the American karate champion. Over and over he repeated how important it was to think about health and fitness. Think about each part of your body, he said, and isolate the individual parts when you exercise. This, he insisted, is the key to good health and longevity.

I don't question the fact that the modern champion's prescription for good health and fitness is sound advice, and I have no doubt that it works for him and his students. Also I know that heredity and environment have a great impact on health and fitness, as do diet and consistency of exercise.

But as I read the champion's words and reflected on Koyama's story, I couldn't stop the words from escaping my lips: "Hang in there, champ."

FOCUS, NOT POWER

A typical public demonstration of karate in the early 1960's consisted of some basic techniques, perhaps a *kata* (formal exercise), some self-defense techniques, and then the piece de resistance: board and brick breaking. The breaking exhibition was what the audience really came to see, and it was what intrigued the performers most, also.

Today, board and brick breaking has been deleted from most demonstrations given by traditional karate practitioners, mainly because they believe the public has been given a false impression by such theatrics. This was already the attitude of the traditionalists by the mid-1960s, but it was an attitude held mostly by the instructors, not the students. We still thrilled at the prospect of seeing our instructor break something, or, even better, having a chance to break something ourselves. Nevertheless, our instructors were firm: we should not give demonstrations of breaking, and we should not enter breaking divisions at tournaments.

One day, at the *dojo* of a prominent Japanese instructor, the subject of breaking came up during a visit from a young Korean instructor who was opening a school in the area. After a brief discussion with the instructor, the young man left for a few minutes and returned with a box full of bricks. We all sat down to watch, and he placed two bricks parallel to each other on a burlap bag lying on the floor. On top of these two bricks, he placed three more, one on top of the other, forming a bridge. After a few more words with the instructor (the discussion, we learned later, was about power), the young man stood in front of his brick bridge in a long, low stance, and breathed deeply several times. After a few moments of deep breathing and concentration, he let out a piercing shout and smacked his forehead down on the bricks, smashing all three into a pile of rubble.

"Can you do this?" he asked our instructor.

"I don't know," Sensei replied, "but wait a moment, please."

Our instructor disappeared into the back room for a minute or two, and when he returned, he brought with him a twelve-inch square board, one inch thick. After rummaging in his desk for a minute, he produced a rubber band and a thumbtack. Securing the rubber band to one edge of the board with the tack, he called on one of his students to hold the other end of the rubber band, suspending the board in midair. Facing the dangling board in a front stance, he extended his clenched fist about six inches from the surface of the board, looked at the young man, and said, "Can you do this?"

With that, he thrust his fist forward six inches, snapping the board in half with a resounding crack, one half flying all the way across the dojo, the other half dangling lightly from the rubber band.

"I don't know," the younger man mumbled, but he made no attempt to duplicate the feat.

Later, our instructor lectured us sternly and carefully. "Power is one thing," he said. "*Kime* (focus) is another."

All of us tried to duplicate the feat later, of course, and we were in fact able to break a suspended board if we punched from the hip and moved very fast. But all attempts to break it with only a six-inch snap of the fist resulted only in bruised knuckles and a broken rubber band.

What our instructor was trying to teach us did not really become clear until a short time later, when Hirokazu Kanazawa, along with three other All-Japan karate champions, stopped in the Midwest during a worldwide tour. In front of several hundred people at a public demonstration, Kanazawa explained in his broken English that karate uses the combined

43

force of the mind and body, and that demonstrations of brute power had little meaning.

To illustrate his point, he, like the young Korean instructor before him, built a bridge of bricks. With the same intense concentration, he struck the bricks with the edge of his hand, neatly halving all three. When the applause died down, he thanked the audience and told them that really any one of them could do the same thing with a proper amount of muscle building and hand conditioning. Karate training, however, could enable them to do much more. It could, he said, enable them to develop their minds to a level that would allow them to control their physical power.

To demonstrate this, Kanazawa placed three more bricks in front of him, but this time he made no bridge. He stacked the bricks on top of each other, flat on the concrete floor.

"Now, using mind," he said, "will put power only in middle brick."

To the astonishment of everyone present, he then struck the bricks as he had struck the first three, and only the middle brick broke! The others remained intact.

Not satisfied, however, Kanazawa then had one of the other instructors toss three one-inch boards into the air, and he broke each one with punches, skeet-shooting style. "This physical," he said. "Only speed. Now show karate mind."

To demonstrate "karate mind," he picked up five boards, placed them together, and had two assistants hold them in place in front of him. Choosing a young man from the audience, Kanazawa asked him, "Which board you like me break?"

"Third one from the front," the young man said.

"Okay," Kanazawa replied. Standing in his long front stance facing the boards, he then breathed deeply, clearing his mind. He punched then, shattering the stillness of the room, and asked the young man to examine the boards. Only the third board from the front was broken!

Kanazawa repeated this feat several times, always asking the audience which board they wanted him to break, and always breaking only that board.

In trying to explain it to us later in the dojo, he fumbled for words. "Just train," he said. "Use mind and body together. Mind can control body. Want to break something, just put mind in thing you want to break; body will follow."

I doubt that many people believe this story when I tell it, but for those of us in that room on that day, it was an event that will never be forgotten. And in Hawaii, where Kanazawa taught for two years, his breaking techniques are legendary.

His explanation was simple: "Focus, not power."

JUSTICE

B lood was everywhere. In shock, I kneeled down and raised the bloodied face of the young Japanese who had been my instructor for the last few months.

"*Sempai* (senior), are you all right?" I asked.

"Yes," he replied weakly. "I think I'll be okay now."

It was an unusual set of circumstances that had brought both of us to this situation. I was a brown belt student without a regular instructor in my city and, along with another brown belt friend of mine, had jumped at the chance to have a Japanese instructor visit us for an extended period. Our chief instructor had called and explained that a young Japanese ranking in the third *dan* was planning to make a tour of the United States, both to gain experience in karate against the larger Americans and to sharpen his teaching skills. He would stay in three or four different cities for two, three, or four months at a time, we were told, and all he needed was a minimal salary and living expenses. Best of all, to our youthful way of thinking, he was the reigning All-Japan Collegiate *Kumite* (sparring) Champion.

I was a high school student at the time, so I had my doubts about being able to raise the necessary money for his visit. But my friend was a few years older and he had a very good job in his family's business, so he determined that he would be able to bear the financial burden.

In seeing a young Japanese champion, we expected to be dazzled by brilliant, flashy moves and extremely powerful techniques, and we were not disappointed. The instructor's starting motion, viewed from straight ahead, was impossible to see. He could stand 10 feet away and literally dash forward, punch me in the stomach, and return to his original position before I could get my hands up to block. His agility was also amazing. Once, when we asked him to help us give a demonstration at a local high school, he jumped over my head and kicked me in the back of the neck on the way down. What made the feat so extraordinary was the fact that we had not planned that movement at all; he just decided on the spot that the audience would like something like that. They certainly did, but it scared me to death.

All of us who were training really grew fond of this extraordinary young man. He was a bit older than we, of course, and he was a graduate of one of Japan's most prestigious universities. When he talked, therefore, we would all gather around in a circle to sit and listen and learn. In our eyes, he could do no wrong.

Near the end of the instructor's four-month stay, however, my friend was called out of town for three days to tend to some business. Not wanting to be away from training for very long, he told me before he left that he thought he might be able to wrap up the business deal in only one or two days and get back home early.

Indeed, he did finish his business in less than two days, and he drove like a madman to get home in time for the Thursday night class. Arriving at his home in mid-afternoon, he was thinking about how surprised his wife would be to see him home so early. When he opened the door to his house, he heard voices in another room, and when he entered the room, there was his wife and our Japanese instructor. To use a polite euphemism, they were in a compromising position.

I don't know exactly why my friend didn't fly into a rage, but he didn't even say a word. With his wife's sputtered explanations ringing in his ears, he calmly turned and silently left the house.

He was waiting for me at my house when I got home from school, and he talked to me as if he were in a daze. He told me what had happened, and he told me that he was going to go to class that night anyway, to see what the instructor's attitude would be. I encouraged him to stay away, but he insisted.

I was a nervous wreck when I got to the dojo, but to my surprise the instructor came in with the same smile he always had, the same formality of demeanor we had grown accustomed to,

and he acted as he always did. During class, he taught as he always had, and he corrected all of us, including my friend, in the manner we had come to admire.

After class, my friend and I got together to talk, and after a long period of uncomfortable silence, he spoke to me in calm, measured tones.

"You know what?" he said evenly. "That man leaves me no choice. I have to challenge him and do my best to beat him into the ground. What do you think?"

"I think he'll kill you!" I shouted. "Man, you don't have a chance in the world against that guy. You've seen him move, and you've even faced him in free sparring a dozen times. He plays with us like we're babies! It would be suicide! Besides, your wife wouldn't have been in that situation with him if she hadn't wanted to. As hard as that is to accept, I think you are going to have to accept it, put it behind you, get a divorce or whatever, and get on with your life. Challenging a guy like the instructor is crazy!"

"I have no choice," he replied calmly.

"Baloney! You have lots of choices. Just walk away! And what would it prove, anyway? You don't have to be a macho man and prove that you can take a beating. That's just plain stupid!"

On and on we went like this for almost two hours, me always trying to take the rational view, and my friend always saying the same thing: "He has offended and challenged my manhood, and I can't live with that. I don't care if he does kill me. If I had to live with the knowledge that I didn't act like a man because I was afraid, I would rather be dead."

No matter how hard I tried, I could not dissuade him from his foolish position. Finally, he said he would issue the challenge on Saturday, and he asked if I would come along to back him up.

"No way!" I responded firmly. "He may be a rotten guy, and he may have offended your sense of manhood, but he hasn't done anything to me, and I don't want to die. I will get the first aid kit in shape, though, and I'll hang around to pick up the pieces, if there are any left."

Following Saturday's class, which went without incident just as Thursday's had, my friend marched into the instructor's office and issued the challenge. He told him that his sense of dignity and morality had been grievously offended, and he said he demanded satisfaction.

The instructor stared at him without expression and then said quietly, "Yes, I understand."

"Meet me in the alley in back!" my friend snapped. Then he spun around and marched out.

I watched as the instructor strode smoothly toward the back door of the dojo, and as soon as he was through it, I grabbed the first aid kit and sat it just inside the door. I stepped out into the alley to see the two of them facing each other about 10 feet apart. My friend had his knees flexed and his hands raised to chest level; the Japanese was standing naturally, hands at his sides.

"You know why I have to do this, don't you?" my friend shouted at him.

The instructor silently nodded in affirmation.

"Put your hands up and fight, you filthy scum!" my friend screamed, but the instructor remained motionless.

"Oh, no," I thought. "My friend is too angry, too full of openings. The instructor will drop him so fast, he won't know what happened."

To my surprise, though, the instructor remained calm and motionless as my friend crept toward him. At the very last instant, when I was sure he would kill my friend with a lashing kick or lightning-fast punch, the instructor did a very odd thing: he closed his eyes.

At that instant, with all the rage and fury of a man whose life has been destroyed, my friend hammered the instructor with a full-force reverse punch to the face. My friend was only a brown belt, but he was very strong, and the small Japanese instructor flew backward about six feet, spinning in the air and

landing on his face in the concrete alleyway. Blood rocketed from his nose from the force of the blow, and his lack of defense surprised my friend so much that he just stood there for a minute with a blank expression on his face.

"Get up, you _____!" he screamed. "Get up!"

Slowly, the Japanese pushed himself up to his knees, and then jumped toward my friend, running like a sprinter just off the starting blocks. Without hesitation, my friend kicked him in the stomach, and dealt two more rapid-fire punches to his face. The Japanese dropped like a stone.

Emotionally out of control now, my friend hovered over him and screamed obscenities, brandishing his fists and admonishing the instructor to get up for more.

"That's enough!" I said loudly. "He's had it."

51

My friend looked at me, then looked down and spit in the bloodied face of the man lying beneath his feet.

When my friend left, I rushed over and raised the head of the instructor. "Sempai, are you all right?" I asked.

"Yes," he replied weakly, "I think I'll be okay now."

I quickly retrieved the first aid kit and began cleaning the cuts on the young man's face. He was a mess: both lips split, a cut on one cheekbone and another over one eyebrow. His nose bled profusely, and was swollen and twisted.

"Sempai, I think your nose is broken, and you might have some broken ribs, too. You'd better let me take you to a hospital."

"No," he said slowly, "I'll be okay."

After about thirty minutes, he turned over and pushed himself to a squatting position, mopping the ooze from his face with a surgical sponge.

"Sempai, " I asked, "why didn't you defend yourself? I saw you close your eyes the first time he hit you, and I saw you run at him with your hands down. You didn't even make an effort to defend yourself, did you?"

"You know," he replied, "Master Funakoshi taught us that if the cause is just, the karateka will go forward into battle against one opponent or 10,000 opponents, and will take no thought for his own safety. This is the way of *budo*. But the reverse is also true. If the cause is not just, we will not fight under any circumstances.

"In this case, your friend's cause was completely just. I did a terrible thing to him, and I deserved to be punished. And he deserved the right of revenge. It's not enough just to say that we want to perfect our character and want to be able to defend ourselves. In this case, I showed that my character still needs a lot of work. I'm ashamed of what I did to him, and I could not have defended myself against him in any case, because he was right and I was wrong. Let's have some tea."

It was a few years later that I read Master Funakoshi's words: "The purpose of karate-do is to train your body and mind every day, and in times of crisis to be utterly committed to the cause of justice."

After watching my senior in the alley that day, I think I know what he meant.

THE BEST PLACE TO TRAIN

The *dojo* has changed a lot in appearance since I began training in the early 1960s. Sometimes I am taken aback when prospective students ask about the facilities at the community education center where I teach.

"Do you have showers?" they want to know. "Sauna? Steam room? Lockers?"

"No," I tell them. "All we have is a *dojo*—two dressing rooms with hooks for your clothes and a training floor. We are lucky enough, however, to have an office."

Some of my more business-minded, lower-ranking students have pointed out to me that I might be losing prospective students by not having more lavish facilities, and I always remind them that a *dojo* is for training and not necessarily for feeling comfortable.

I know it must be hard for some modern students to comprehend, but the first *dojo* I trained in was a smallish, rectangular room which had a front door, a back door, a toilet, and no windows. The floor was rough concrete that had never seen tile, and there were no dressing rooms. There was a bamboo blind on the front door, and since the back door led to an alley, we saw no reason for dressing rooms until a couple of women decided to join. Then we put nails in the woodwork and strung a curtain along some wire that somebody found in the trunk of his car. The facilities were hardly in a league with Vic Tanny or Jack LaLanne. The monthly fee was $12, and since there were about 13 or 14 of us training at that time, the instructor was usually able to pay the rent with only a little extra cash from his pocket.

I really have to think hard to remember details like these, because they are overshadowed in my mind by the incredibly good education I received at that place. Boy, did we ever train! Seven days a week we entered that sweatbox and learned more about karate than we ever guessed existed.

I don't mean to be a curmudgeon here, but my point is that I think a lot of the more meaningful values of karate-do are obscured today by the need to succeed in business. There certainly is nothing wrong with having a spacious, beautiful *dojo* replete with the latest training devices, and at my age, I would be the last to negate the marvelous feeling of sliding into a whirlpool after two or three hours of rigorous training. But how do all these modern conveniences affect the attitudes of today's karate students?

One very positive effect, from the viewpoint of the instructor and the manufacturers and promoters of martial arts supplies, is that people are much more likely to be attracted to lavish surroundings than to dimly lit rooms which smell something like the reptile house at the local zoo. No argument there; I feel the same way.

Another positive factor is that modern psychologists have clearly shown that people's ability to learn is directly influenced by their surroundings. We even have good information exploring the effects of various colors on the learning process. And there can be no doubt that it just makes good business sense to have a pleasant place in which to conduct business.

So what, you might ask, is my problem with beautiful, modern karate studios? No problem at all, except that I'm not convinced they represent

the backbone of real karate-do. Some of them fall into that category, of course, because of their excellent instructors. But the backbone of karate-do, as I have observed it, is more likely to be found in garages, basements, YMCAs and, yes, even in dimly lit rooms that smell like a reptile refuge.

Some of the most spirited karate training I have ever witnessed occurs regularly near my home in a spare room of an armory. The room is concrete from top to bottom and has no windows. When I visited there recently, I saw 20 or 30 students training as hard as human beings can train—training so hard, in fact, that the perspiration from their bodies was collecting on the low, concrete ceiling and dripping on them. Not Vic Tanny's, but excellent karate.

Another place I visit from time to time sits out in the country, in a field where the world's largest mosquitoes and horseflies go to breed. The place used to be a church, and the wood floor still has holes in it where the pews used to be fastened. There are six lights in the ceiling, but only two of them burn, and there is only one electrical outlet. The number of outlets is of no consequence, because a fuse blows every time anything like a fan is plugged in. In this place, three times a week, one can observe 20 or more people in their white *gi*, punching, striking, kicking and blocking, apparently oblivious to the extreme Midwest heat and humidity. Really excellent karate.

I regularly teach in places like these, and until a friend pointed it out to me a short time ago, I didn't realize how jaded I was to the poor training facilities. These are the kinds of places where I learned karate, and it is just natural, I suppose, that I would think they are wonderful, horseflies and mosquitoes notwithstanding.

But to get back to my original point—psychologists and business sense also notwithstanding—I wonder about the effects of the training environment on the individual student of karate. It seems to me that the training environment indicates to the student, mostly subconsciously, what he or she should expect from training. If the surroundings are lavish and comfortable, the student can reasonably expect a good return on his investment of money in the studio. That is, he can expect certain treatment and cordialities from his instructor and classmates. A modern, high-tech atmosphere is, after all, a classy atmosphere. Everything should be bright, cheerful, and should smell good—including the instructor and classmates. Whether he is ready to admit it or not, the proprietor of such a studio is also influenced by the surroundings so as to conduct business in a modern, professional manner.

If, on the other hand, the environment is plain, unadorned and simple, the student expects to be treated in a plain, unadorned fashion. When the *dojo* is a simple, clean room, the instructor can tell the students, "We do only one thing here: we practice karate."

I don't know which environment is best for learning, but I do know one thing for sure. Those people who are training in the armory in pools of their own sweat, and those who are practicing with the horseflies and mosquitoes are there for only one reason: they want to learn karate. Unless they are masochists, their only attraction to those places is the opportunity to learn karate under a good instructor.

So I admire those instructors who reside in lavish studios and still manage to teach good karate to their students. But I loudly applaud those who work so hard, day after day, in the often not too comfortable surroundings of old churches, armories, garages, and basements. They are the backbone of true karate-do, and they teach and practice for only one reason: they sincerely want to learn karate-do.

They have no other motive.

A TRUE MASTER

In the course of karate training, one has good days and bad days. At the beginning and intermediate levels, when students are still trying to impress their peers, it seems like one person's voice always rises above the din of the locker room after a training session. It is the voice of the lucky guy who had an exceptionally good day and was rewarded with the teacher's attention. His moment in the sun is always fleeting, and he generally takes advantage of it quickly and loudly. At least that's the way things worked in most of the *dojo* I trained in.

It is an exercise in pure egotism.

Such moments were rare for me, so I was doubly pleased when my chance came some time ago on one hot, July day. I was preparing to test for black belt, and my spirit was very high. Disregarding the humid, 104-degree Midwestern heat, the teacher pushed us hard for more than two hours.

The class began with hundreds of kicks and punches, followed by intense semi-free sparring with the emphasis on a new and difficult shifting maneuver. It seemed that everyone was struggling and stumbling—everyone but me. I was performing as if I had invented the maneuver. Even after spirit training— 1,000 kicks with each leg, 100 sit-ups, 200 punches on the *makiwara*, 15 laps around the *dojo*—I felt fresh and energetic.

One of my seniors took notice of my energy, and he grabbed me by the arm immediately after class. "Let's spar for a while," he said.

Such an invitation by this particular senior was ordinarily not a coveted item. At six feet, three-and-one-half inches and

190 pounds, he was a giant in my eyes. My five-foot, six-inch, 130-pound frame was dwarfed by comparison. Not only that, but I was a brown belt, and he ranked in the second *dan*. We had a saying about him: "His arms are so long, I'll bet he can roll up his socks without bending over."

Nevertheless, on this particular day, I felt no fear, and it was a strange, new sensation for me.

We faced each other in the middle of the floor and bowed, and I immediately charged forward, propelled by a loud *kiai*, and punched him solidly in the chest. To my complete astonishment, he staggered backward and looked surprised. "Oh, boy," I thought. "That was the dumbest thing I've ever done. He'll kill me for sure now."

Again to my surprise, he didn't kill me at all. He charged toward me with one of his long legs lashing out in a front kick, but I magically shifted just to the side and punched him the chest again. As he recovered, I drove my body forward, punching and kicking, and he actually retreated! "Incredible!" I thought. "Nobody has ever made him back up before!"

While this was flashing through my mind, our teacher suddenly yelled, "Stop!" Looking back at the incident now, I real-

ize he probably stopped it before my senior became enraged and seriously injured me.

"Just like a tournament," our instructor said. "You two fight. I'll referee and call points."

We bowed again and circled each other cautiously. When I had faced my senior in the past, I had been filled with fear. But this time, it was as if there was a bright light illuminating his vital areas. All I could see was the "target" of his face, neck, and midsection.

He feinted with his front hand, and I drove in hard, slamming my fist into his belly and screaming a *kiai* from the bottom of my soul.

"*Waza-ri!*" the instructor shouted, indicating I had scored a half point. "*Tzukete hajime!*" he shouted. "Begin again!"

This time, my senior really charged fast and hard. As he did, I deftly shifted just out of his reach and, with my forward leg, snapped a roundhouse kick to his throat.

"Enough!" our teacher yelled. "Very good!"

We bowed, and my senior put his arm around me, squeezed my neck and grinned. "You little son of a gun!" he said. "I didn't think you had it in you."

What a joy it was to strut into the locker room while all the other students dragged! My best friend, a student of equal rank, slumped on the bench in a sweating stupor while I bounced around the room, expounding, bragging, and explaining the details of techniques to all present, whether they wanted to hear it or not.

My friend slumped, expressionless, and said nothing.

For five or 10 minutes I continued. Still jabbering, I yanked off my belt and jacket, dropping my towel on the floor. As I stooped down to retrieve it, I cracked my forehead hard on a protruding clothes hook. Stunned, I bounced backward onto the bench a few feet from my friend. Seriously dazed, I sat motionless for several minutes. Gradually I became aware of blood trickling from my forehead and running down to my chin. Slowly, I turned toward my friend.

Still expressionless, he sighed, "Yeah, a true master."

STARTING OVER

I knew it was going to be a bad day as soon as I bowed. "No! Start over!" my teacher barked. I thought, Start over? All I did was bow!

The situation took place years ago, and my teacher, a great master, had traveled several thousand miles to see my students for the first time since I had opened my own *dojo*. I was surprised that, in front of my students, he treated me with great deference, as if I were a peer. For the first two days, he buttressed my confidence, talked intimately with me, and stroked my ego. By the second day of his visit, my ego was riding high on a wave of thick pride.

On the third and final day of his visit, he announced that we would each perform our favorite kata under his attentive and critical eye.

"You first," he said, pointing at me. "Everyone warm up."

Since I badly lacked regular instruction, I was ecstatic over the prospect of having my teacher give me a private lesson.

Standing on the floor in front of him, with all my students' eyes trained on me, I was ready to give them a show—to show them the excellence of my techniques. They would see why I had risen to a position of such high esteem in the eyes of the great master.

"Start over!" he growled. "You have no *zanshin*! Where is your spirit?"

My thought was one of embarrassment. Oh, well. My students probably wouldn't even remember such a minor error. But after bowing for the fifth time, I forgot about my students.

I even forgot about the whir of the movie camera recording the fiasco. All I could hear was my instructor's harsh scolding. He and I were the only two people in existence, and my only desire was to perform the first movement of the *kata*.

"*Hai*! First movement! One!" he shouted.

Grateful for my release from torture, I performed that movement as it had never been performed before—smooth, graceful, flowing, strong, full of feeling and intensity. I could see an opponent in my mind's eye, and I could see him withering under the onslaught of my excellent technique.

"Oh, oh, oh," my teacher said, shaking his head sadly. "No," he said, adjusting my head. "No," he said, adjusting my arms. "no, no, no." He continued with my shoulders, my back, my legs, my knees, my feet and my toes. Finally, he kicked my rump and whacked my belly hard.

"Start over!"

And so it went, over and over, again and again, through each movement of the *kata*: me performing the movement endlessly, and my instructor whacking, smacking, thumping, and scolding. I must have completed each movement of that *kata* at least 10 or 15 times. As soon as I was able to perform it with some semblance of correctness, he would whack me and thump me again, shouting in my ear, "Start over!" And back to the beginning of the *kata* I would go.

For 45 minutes, we continued. No rest.

I'm going to pass out, I thought.

"Start over!"

I can't breathe!

"Start over!"

I can't see him! Where did he go?

"Start over!"

Suddenly I knew it. I knew it as well as I knew my own name: If he said "start over" just one more time, I would expire. I was going to die, and I didn't care. Anything would be better than this.

"*Hai*! Finished! Bow!" His voice came as gentle rain on a parched desert. It was over.

As I staggered toward the side of the floor, I saw the awed faces of my students staring at me, mouths agape. They were staring at the redness in my face, and they seemed perplexed by my ragged gasps for air.

They will probably all quit, I thought, now that they have seen how lousy I really am.

Then my teacher walked over to me, turning his back to the other students so they could not see his face. He patted me on the back, smiled, and very quietly, so no one else could hear, said, "Very good *kata*. I'm proud of you."

Returning his face to its steely scowl, he turned toward my students and shouted, "Next!"

IF IT'S NON-CONTACT, HOW DO YOU KNOW IT WILL WORK?

Ever since I walked into a karate *dojo* many years ago, I have heard the following question debated in many forms: "If you guys don't make contact, how do you know your techniques will work against an actual opponent?"

When I was younger, I entered into this debate with vigor. I smashed the *makiwara* (padded punching board) with all my might, and I sometimes broke some boards or bricks to demonstrate the power of karate punches, strikes, or kicks. But I only did this once in front of my teacher, because when he witnessed my egotistic antics, he berated me and literally beat large lumps and bruises on tender parts of my body.

"That is stupid!" he would rave. "The purpose of karate-do is to build character, not to prove who is the strongest or toughest. It doesn't matter who is the strongest or toughest. It doesn't matter who is strongest or who can beat up whom!"

But to my youthful way of thinking and, I suspect, the thinking of the majority of young people who take up the study of karate, it did matter. It mattered a great deal.

Now that I am older, I of course agree with my teacher. I teach my own students that toughness and strength are of no consequence. I honestly tell them that I don't practice karate-do so that I will be able to beat up my enemies. I tell them that there are undoubtedly people around who could come blindfolded into my *dojo*, hands tied behind their backs, with their feet stuck in a bucket, yet they could beat me senseless without working up a sweat. And I tell them that this doesn't matter.

But when I was a teenager, it mattered. In fact, I remember the exact instant when it ceased to matter, the same instant in which I ceased trying to explain how I knew non-contact karate would work in a real situation.

It happened in the mid-1960s when karate was still a relatively new thing in America—a time when karate tournaments were largely a last-minute hodgepodge mixture of every Japanese and Okinawan style imaginable. When all these different styles got together, the leaders would sit down for a few minutes and agree in principle on the rules of the event. Detailed rules were left to the innovative discretion of the referee and judges during the contest.

I had fought in many tournaments as a white and green belt, but this tournament was something special. People were there from all over the Midwest, and some of the biggest names in early-60s karate were there to judge. A couple of them even entered the black belt sparring division.

The prospect of facing some of those big names, even though I was sure I would lose, excited my competitive brown belt soul. After much haggling and outright begging, I was allowed to compete in the black belt division. The tournament director seemed amused at the thought of a brown belt trying to compete against the black belts.

"Sure," he grinned. "Have at it."

The only rules that seemed etched in granite were no contact to the face, and no open-hand techniques to the face. A minor infraction of either of these rules would result in a warning, and two warnings would result in a foul and disqualification.

My first two matches went well, I thought, and I was surprised that I won them. My third opponent, however, was something else.

As I stepped into the ring, I found my five-foot, six-inch, 130-pound self facing a six-foot, three-inch, 180-pound ogre. He was an Okinawan stylist who apparently was more than a little miffed at the sight of this cocky little brown belt beating up on black belts. He glared and frowned at me, and to this day, I'm sure I heard him growl.

My teacher, it should be noted, had refused to participate in this tournament in any way. He didn't approve of "open" tournaments where the rules were not fixed beforehand. He had told me he did not want me to participate in this "circus," as he called it, but that if I insisted, he would go along to watch and take me to the hospital if necessary.

As I looked at the giant in front of me, I was pierced by cold fear. As I looked beyond him, I saw my teacher taking up a seat on the sidelines, folding his arms across his chest and staring at me with no expression at all. He knew what I did not know at the time: the referee of the match was my opponent's instructor, a man who also was not pleased that a brown belt was denigrating the black belt division.

As the match began, I dashed forward instantly and planted a reverse punch squarely in my opponent's chest. To my amazement, the referee said nothing. As the match continued, the big guy moved this way and that, punching and kicking almost continuously with his front leg. As he raised his leg for yet another kick, I shifted inside, grabbed his leg at the calf, and punched him solidly in the chest. The force of my blow, coupled with a heavy tug on his leg, sent him reeling backward onto the floor.

"Half-point!" said the referee disgustedly. Then he walked up to the face of my opponent and said something to him that was inaudible to anyone else.

"Continue!" he shouted.

Again, I dashed in with a punch to the chest, but no point followed. I punched once more, a little harder, but again the referee made no move to call a point. I looked at the referee, and he just glared at me with a smirk on his face. That smirk told me the whole story. There was no way I could win this match.

Angered by this blatant "fix," I charged my opponent with all my might. In a rage, I grabbed his uniform near his collarbone, and I punched him three or four times in rapid succession, very hard.

"Stop!" commanded the referee.

As I let go and dropped my hands, my opponent lashed out with an open-hand attack directly to my face. I think it was a palm heel, but I half turned and half ducked, and it caught me square on the side of the head, between my left ear and temple. As I spun around, he kicked out at me, landing a hard strike to the inside of my left thigh, narrowly missing my groin.

"Okay," the referee said.

I staggered back to my starting position and instantly became aware of three things: I could not hear out of my left ear, I could not see out of my left eye, and blood was gushing from my right nostril. The man had hit me so hard on the left side of the head that blood was coming out of the right side of my nose!

As the referee prepared to motion for us to continue, I held out my right hand covered with blood and looked at him incredulously.

"Oh," he said with nonchalance. "You want to quit?"

Stunned, I looked past him with my good eye and looked directly into the eyes of my teacher. With a sigh and a shrug of his shoulders, my teacher looked directly up at the ceiling, then back at me, and then at his hands, as if he were checking his manicure.

"No way!" I replied, wiping the blood on my gi jacket.

"One warning for showing disrespect to an official," the referee announced, pointing at me.

I bowed to him and faced the monster again. This time, as he moved forward, he did so with a very hard kick that caught me again high on the inside of the thigh. As he put his leg down, I grabbed his jacket and punched him hard in the face and harder in the body. As he reeled backward, I swept his feet from under him and hit him hard on the back of the head, bouncing his forehead against the wood floor of the gymnasium.

"Foul!" cried the referee, and it was over.

It took almost 30 minutes for my nosebleed to stop, and I couldn't hear out of my left ear for more than two hours. My eye turned very black and remained that way for almost two weeks.

My opponent, as it turned out, suffered a broken tooth and three broken ribs.

"And what do you feel now?" my teacher asked as I reached the sidelines.

"Ashamed," I replied, mopping blood and trying to feel if my left eye was indeed still there.

"And why did you not kill him?" he asked.

Shocked by his unusual question, I replied quickly, "Oh, I didn't want to kill him. I just wanted to get even. It wasn't fair."

"Hmm," said my teacher. "Maybe you are not so stupid anymore." And he walked away.

I tell this story now with the shame and guilt of youthful miscarriage, because it is something I would never do now and would not sanction the same for my own students.

But in that place, at that time, I realized that my opponent and I could just as easily have killed each other. As it was, we just made fools of ourselves. But when we hear the question now, "How do you know it will work?" we just smile and say nothing.

AN EXERCISE IN HEAD SHRINKING

A very old Japanese maxim informs us, "The swiftest sword is the one that is never drawn." I mulled over this particular proverb for many years, unsuccessfully trying to decipher it and apply it to my training. It seemed awfully obscure to me, and I had pretty much given up on discerning its meaning until about two years ago.

During a conversation, Teruyuki Okazaki, Chairman and Chief Instructor of the International Shotokan Karate Federation, told me a story that finally gave me an insight, and I think his story bears repeating.

"From the instant that Master Funakoshi promoted me to black belt," Okazaki recalled, "my head began to grow. I was young, impetuous, and overloaded with ego. Shortly after my black belt examination, Mr. Nakayama, who was Funakoshi's assistant, told me to go to one end of the gym and teach a group of beginners their first lesson. What an ego trip that was! After all those years of being a student, I was finally going to be able to get even by showing these beginners how good I was.

"When I got to the other end of the gym, I was surprised to see Master Funakoshi sitting on the side in a chair. 'This is wonderful,' I thought. 'He will be proud to see what a good black belt I am!'

"I started the class, and immediately began yelling at the new students. 'No, no, no!' I shouted. 'That's terrible! Do it this way! Shut up; don't ask foolish questions!'

"After several minutes of this, I heard a small, frail voice calling my name. 'Okazaki,' it called gently, 'come here for a moment.' With great surprise, I suddenly realized it was Funakoshi calling me. He wants to congratulate me on my stern teaching method, I thought.

"I ran to him and bowed deeply. 'Yes, sir!' I shouted.

"'Are you a black belt?' he asked in his high, whining voice.

"'I beg your pardon, sir?'

"'Are you a black belt?' he repeated.

"'Oh, yes, sir! I'm Okazaki. You promoted me at the last examination.

"'Who promoted you?' he asked incredulously.

"'Why, you did, sir. You remember me. I'm Okazaki!'

"Master Funakoshi was about ninety years old at that time, and I was beginning to think he had taken leave of his senses or, at the very least, his memory.

"'No,' he said, 'I don't think so, but maybe you can help me remember. Show me your punch.'

"Stepping back from him, I began punching slowly in the air.

"'Is that how a black belt punches, Okazaki?' he asked. 'I thought black belts were supposed to be strong and fast.'

"'Of course, sir!' I shouted. And I began punching faster and harder.

"'Tsk, tsk,' he clucked, shaking his head derisively. 'That's a terrible punch. You couldn't possibly be a black belt. You couldn't do any damage to anybody.'

"'Yes I could!' I shouted, now verging on a fit of temper. I also realized that everybody in the gym had stopped practicing, and they were all staring at me.

"'Then show me!' Funakoshi shouted. 'Go ahead; try to punch me! You're so weak, I don't think you can do it!'

"I was young and foolish, and my embarrassment turned into a blind rage. I charged at him, screaming my *kiai* from the pit of my stomach. I punched at him with all my might, squinting my eyes and baring my teeth.

"As the thunder of my scream died slowly in the old gym, I gradually realized that Funakoshi was no longer there. It was like waking from a bad dream, realizing that what was so real the instant before was just a figment of imagination. But as I straightened up, I thought, 'This is no dream! This is the *dojo*! Where did he go? Did I imagine this?'

"'Okazaki,' the small voice said from behind me. I jumped as if the Devil himself had jabbed me in the rear with his pitchfork. Funakoshi was standing about 10 feet behind me, smiling calmly!

"'You missed, Okazaki,' he said gently, walking toward me. 'You have all this strength and all this fine technique, but you can't even punch a little 90-year-old man. Perhaps you should remember this and treat the young students with respect and compassion, so that when you are old and frail like me, they won't beat you up. Now please continue teaching your class.'

"No experience in my life has even come close to terrifying me like that one did. I still don't understand how that 90-year-old man could end up behind me without me seeing him move. But I do understand one thing: having a big ego and the big head that goes with it is the most foolish and dangerous thing a human being can possess.

"When I think about how Funakoshi shrunk my big head down to size, I think it's a wonder I have a head at all.

RE-LEARNING AN OLD LESSON

Readers of this column sometimes write to me and say that what I have written has helped them gain some insight into their art. This is always gratifying, and would make my head increase three hat sizes if it were not for the readers who write to say that they appreciate my column because it saves them money on birdcage liners. The pages on which my column are printed, they suggest, have more uses than are readily apparent to the casual reader. I appreciate all these letters because they force me to take my work seriously.

But I never dreamed until just recently that I would learn something from one of my own columns, yet that is exactly what happened.

I was sitting around feeling sorry for myself, you see. A painful, recurring injury was plaguing me, and I was questioning why I do what I do, and how I could possibly go on. My schedule, it seemed, was terrible, and I was bemoaning the fact that a man my age would be so foolish as to get himself into this situation.

A mental inventory of my situation did not make me feel any better: I teach a class four times a week at 8:00 a.m. I also teach two classes on Monday nights and three classes on Tuesday nights. And then I drive 65 miles each way to teach two classes on Wednesday nights. Besides that, I teach three classes on Thursday nights, and I drive 50 miles each way to teach two classes on Friday nights. Additionally, I teach two classes on Saturday afternoons. About once a month, I travel by plane to conduct clinics and special training seminars. And this isn't even what I do for a living! For a livelihood, I write books and articles and am a book editor.

And here you are sitting in pain, I thought. How about a social life? How about a vacation? How about some fun? Nobody can keep this pace.

In the midst of my reverie, just as I was deciding that bowling would be a suitable exercise substitute for karate, the phone rang, It was a call informing me that the final itinerary had been set for the visit of Masatoshi Nakayama, headmaster of the Japan Karate Association. Nakayama, then in his 70s, was scheduled to visit North America on a teaching tour from late May through early August, under the sponsorship of Teruyuki Okazaki and the International Shotokan Karate Federation (ISKF). On Nakayama's last tour two years earlier, he traveled and taught at a pace that would kill the average man, not to mention a man in his 70s.

But he won't be visiting as many places this time, I was told. After all, he is not a young man, and we don't want him to get too tired. In fact, from the time Nakayama lands in Seattle, he

will only be going to Vancouver, Winnipeg, St. Paul, Denver, Sioux Falls, St. Louis, Philadelphia, Toronto, Ottawa, Montreal, Boston, Bermuda, Jamaica, San Juan, Barbados, Port of Spain, Georgetown (Guyana), back to Port of Spain, St. Vincent, back to Barbados, New York City, back to Philadelphia, and then to Los Angeles before he returns home to Tokyo in early August.

During this time, he will be teaching, demonstrating, lecturing, examining, and officiating at tournaments. Not only that, but he will teach every day and every night at the ISKF's week-long summer camp in Pennsylvania.

You bet, I thought. We certainly wouldn't want to wear him out!

Ever alert to the possibility of a column or article, I went to my files to see what I had written about Nakayama during his last visit, and there, in my own column, I relearned a valuable lesson.

I reread the words of Shojiro Koyama, explaining how Nakayama was able to keep his killing pace. First, said Koyama, he devoted 100 percent of his energies to the task at hand, never dividing his concentration among many tasks. Whether he was eating, relaxing, teaching, or practicing, he concentrated fully on whatever he was doing at the moment. Second, he had a deep spiritual reserve that was forged on the anvil of rigorous training and also during a walking trek through Outer Mongolia many years ago. And finally, he practiced karate every day, no matter what.

Instantly I realized that I was doing everything wrong. I was sitting around, dividing my attention among many things so that none of them was being accomplished effectively. Instead of training and concentrating, I was sitting there fretting about my minor pain and letting my ego run wild.

Even though I am little more than half of Nakayama's age, I'm very sure that I still wouldn't want to follow him around during his whole tour. I don't think I'm strong enough to take that.

But I do think I might write a letter to myself, thanking me for renewed insight into an old lesson.

KARATE NI SENTE NASHI

arate ni sente nashi ("There is no first attack in karate") is Gichin Funakoshi's most often quoted and least understood maxim. Like most things, I gained some understanding of this principle by observing my seniors and by questioning my teachers.

When I was a brown belt, I thought I had the statement figured out, and I didn't like it much. It meant, I thought, that the karate-ka was never supposed to make the first move, no matter what. Because of his skill, he was supposed to let the enemy attack first and then defend himself. This notion died right after one of my seniors was mugged.

My senior (we'll call him Smith) was on his way home from the *dojo* one night when he was accosted by a youth wielding a billy club. Since Smith's car was in the shop at the time, he was forced to walk three miles to the school, which was in a very run-down part of town.

As he was walking, his would-be mugger stopped him, brandished a weapon, and demanded that Smith turn over his billfold. My senior politely but firmly declined to do so and stood ready to defend himself. As the youth swung his club in a roundhouse fashion, Smith blocked and counter-punched. The mugger dropped like a stone, but the force of Smith's block dislodged the weapon from the attacker's hand, and as luck would have it, the club flew hard against Smith's cheekbone. Nothing was broken, but his face was severely bruised, and for several weeks Smith had to answer the inevitable question, "Gee, what does the other guy look like?"

Some of us were discussing the incident in the *dojo* when our instructor walked by. Praising Smith's courage and ability, we applauded the fact that he was able to defend himself so well.

"You must be proud of him," one of my friends said to the teacher. "He controlled the situation very well."

"Stupid, stupid, stupid!" our instructor spat out in his broken English.

"But he defended himself well, didn't he?"

"No, no, no!" he raged. "This is a terrible example of self-defense. Smith-san not understand anything! He's just stupid! Let bad guy hit him like *makiwara* (punching board).

"Stupid, stupid, stupid," he muttered as he walked away.

None of us could figure it out. We just couldn't understand our teacher's attitude, so we decided to drop the subject of Smith's encounter.

About a year later, I was invited by another of my seniors (we'll call him Jones) to double date for a movie and dinner. After a pleasant meal, we were walking with our dates to a theater that was located on one of the busiest streets in the city. Suddenly, from out of the crowd there appeared a very big, very loud fellow who began shouting obscenities at my senior. The dispute, it seemed, was over the validity of Jones accompanying the young woman he was escorting that night. It turned out the loudmouth had been dating this woman for several years, but they had recently come to an unfriendly parting of the ways.

She was "his girl," the troublemaker was screaming, and he was calling into question the bloodline of Jones' entire family.

My senior quietly and patiently told the guy to calm down, that there was no point in making trouble, and that the woman had a right to date anybody she pleased. He then got close to the man and said very quietly, "Why don't you go down the street and bother somebody else?"

As the loudmouth continued to shout, Jones turned to me and my date and said, "Let's get out of here."

Since the loudmouth was pressing him very hard, I thought it odd that Jones turned his back on the guy to talk to us. Sure enough, just as my friend spoke to us, the troublemaker took a step toward him with his right hand raised. My impression was not that he was going to hit Jones. It seemed, rather, that he was going to grab him by the shoulder and spin him around.

But his intentions became irrelevant when, much to my surprise, Jones spun around with blinding speed, uttered a fierce *kiai*, and planted the hardest reverse punch imaginable in the loudmouth's face. The force of the blow snapped the

man's head back and lifted him off the ground. He appeared literally to fly through the air, spinning as he flew, and landed face down on the concrete pavement with a sickening thud. He wasn't quite unconscious, because he rolled over on his back and groaned, clutching at his face, which was bleeding profusely.

"Now," Jones said quietly, again turning to us, "we can go to the movies." And he walked away, leaving the loudmouth rolling on the ground.

As this story got around the *dojo*, we all were certain that our instructor would be furious with Jones. He had a rule in his dojo that anyone caught fighting in anything less than an unavoidable self-defense situation would be expelled.

Inevitably, however, he caught a few of us discussing the incident, and we abruptly stopped talking when he approached.

"It's O. K.," he said. "I know all about it."

"Are you going to expel Jones-san?" some fool asked.

"Expel?" the teacher replied quizzically. "Why expel?"

"Uh, well, we just thought that the rule against fighting..."

"Rule say," he interjected, "anybody who fights when he can avoid, or anybody start fight, that person expelled. Jones-san O. K. He not start fight. He tried to avoid, had no choice. Must fight. Did good job."

"But," I asked, "Jones-san hit him first. What about *karate ni, sente nashi*?

"Ah, see," he replied, "you are stupid like Smith-san. Smith-san waited for guy to swing stick, and he get hit. First attack is not physical. First attack come when bad guy asked for wallet. Smith-san have bad strategy. He waited for guy's second attack. Jones-san, however, realize that first attack was when guy jumped out and started cussing. He tried to talk him out of it, but guy insisted on fighting. Jones-san just use good strategy: turn back and get bad guy off guard, then counter-attack. One punch, fight over. Question is not 'what is *karate ni sente nashi*?' Question is, 'what is first attack?' Jones-san very smart. He understood. Do you understand?"

"Yes, Sensei!" I shouted.

Actually, I didn't understand at all, but I think I do now.

SECRET ARTS

One of my more esteemed colleagues, Dale F. Poertner, is President of Focus Publications in St. Louis. He is a literate, urbane man who holds degrees in both English literature and library science. He has also been a serious student of Asian culture and Eastern philosophy for more than a quarter of a century, and as an editor and reviewer, he has few peers. He also has no training of any kind in any martial art.

Recently, I was venting my spleen to him about what I saw as the sorry state of modern martial arts in America. I was in a bad mood, and I was decrying the seeming utter lack of respect shown by so many modern martial artists for the traditions of the past. I was saying how terrible it was for people to study an art for a few years and then set themselves up as masters. Not only that, I moaned, but some people are making up *kata* as they go along, and some are even putting this choreography to music. Still others are making up new arts and styles, and a few are going as far as creating lineages on paper to support the validity of their made-up arts. Nothing could be worse, I emphasized, for the public image of the martial arts, as we are being turned into a freak show where the participants seem to know no limits to the depths of bad taste. From outlandish costumes to comic *kata* routines, I concluded, the world of karate is falling apart.

"Nonsense," he replied. "It's the American way. In fact, in America, it's the only way to go, and I say no one has yet gone far enough. I think the ties to the Orient should be broken completely at every level. Then and only then can truly American aesthetics of karate-do be born. What we need are truly American arts with truly American *kata*."

And who, I asked, was going to take the lead in creating these arts?

"Why, me, of course," he answered. "I'm an independent American businessman, and I've thought this through and intend to introduce a series of American arts and *kata* in the very near future."

And what, I asked, are these "arts" to be called?

"Well, first of all," he replied, "there would be the art of *Atache-do*, the art of blocking and attacking with attaché cases. Only two belts will be awarded—black and brown. Belts will be leather for upper ranks, plastic for lower. Another purely American art will be called *Tomat-do*, which we translate as 'way of the way of death.' It will feature attacking with killer tomatoes, but will also include weapons like catsup bottles. All practitioners will wear red belts, with the number of seeds denoting rank."

I don't recall exactly what I said to him, but it had something to do with lack of intellect and taste.

His plans for the new-wave martial arts are not limited to two, he continued. "There won't be any problem attracting the intelligentsia. We'll hit them with *Shamat-do*. In this one, the students who master the rules of chess will be entitled to wear the black and white checkered belt. Beginners will only learn checkers, and they will wear the red and black checkered belt. These arts will reach every level of American society—something for everyone."

And did he, I asked, have any of the technical details of these "arts" worked out?

"Absolutely," he replied with authority. "I haven't worked out the exact placement of the *kata* according to the art, of course, but I'm an American. I know a good thing when I see

it, and musical *kata* is a good thing. All these arts will rely heavily on musical forms like 'The Loan Arranger,' which is a 'seated at desk' *kata*, demonstrating ways to ward off importuning borrowers. It will be performed to a recording of 'Money, Money, Money' from 'Cabaret.'

"*Tanto-tonto* will be a short knife and hatchet weapons *kata* done very quickly to music from the 'William Tell Overture.' Mistakes in this form will cause deep slashes in the limbs, which should pack houses from Baltimore to Seattle.

"Pizzi *kata* will feature many short, sharp hand movements around the upper body. It will be a very strenuous kata done to the music of the 'Pizzicato Polka' by Strauss.

"Basho/hoppu *kata* will draw from the arts of tai chi, *bokken*, and the American ambiance of the 1960s. It will feature side kicks and hops done to Peter, Paul and Mary's 'I'm In Love with a Big Blue Frog.'

"Particularly appropriate for overweight or elderly people will be Sesshin *kata*, a 'no body movement' form. Sesshin will consist of two straight weeks of sitting. No music, no *kiai* (shouting). I think this one will be a rarely performed *kata*.

"And of course we want to appeal to everyone who is already into physical fitness, so we will have a 'Dumbbell' *kata*, with merely grunts instead of *kiai*, performed to the Beatles' 'You Gotta Carry That Weight.'

"For the Bruce Lee aficionados, we will have Kato *kata*, done in black leather clothes and cap while wearing a black mask. It will emphasize steering wheel blocks and kicks, and will be done to 'Flight of the Bumblebee.'

"Finally, the form that I think will be most performed will be the Kamikaze *kata*. This can best be described as a form for the injury-prone. The final movement involves hurling oneself into a wall. Points will be awarded for landing flat on the floor and for unconsciousness. This one will be done to Perez Prado's 'Cherry Pink and Apple Blossom White.' "

"Disgusting," I sighed. "Absolutely disgusting and tasteless."

"Don't hand me that," he snapped. "I've watched modern karate tournaments. This stuff will sell. It will sell big."

The worst part is, I think he might be right.

KARA AND *KU*

Prior to 1936, the Japanese calligraphy representing karate was written with a character for *kara*, also pronounced "T'ang" or "*to*," which referred to the T'ang Dynasty of China. *Te* means "hands." Thus, karate was the art of "Chinese hands." But Gichin Funakoshi, the man who brought karate to Japan from Okinawa, decided that the Okinawans had been too anxious to call the art Chinese, and that it had become clearly Japanese in nature. Additionally, Funakoshi steadfastly maintained that karate was a *do*, a path to follow for a correct, rewarding, and fulfilling life.

In an effort to correct the interpretation of karate as a Chinese art, and at the same time to more clearly indicate the nature of the art as a way of life, Funakoshi changed the character for *kara* from T'ang to *ku*. *Ku* is also pronounced "*kara*" and is found in the *Hannya Shingyo*, a Buddhist sutra containing the phrase *shiki soku ze ku, ku soku ze shiki*. Summarizing the essence and way of life of karate-do, the phrase literally means "Form becomes emptiness, emptiness becomes form."

Shiki is the visible, physical form of a thing. It is the outward appearance of anything, such as a technique or a *kata*. *Ku* is a term similar to the *mu* of *mushin*, and it means "emptiness." But *mu* is a specific term relating to the mind's thinking processes, while *ku* refers more generally to the state of being, without any regard to form. *Ku* acknowledges existence, but describes an absence of form in that existence.

Ku is difficult to describe, but easy to feel. For example, as we go about our daily business, concentrating on our work or studies or whatever, there is a larger process occurring all around us, which we never examine, but which we notice and accept. That larger process is the change of the seasons. As spring turns to summer, the weather becomes warmer, so that one day we notice it is uncomfortably hot outside. As summer turns to fall and then winter, we become aware of the changes in temperature, and suddenly we realize that it  is cold. If we go to bed on a clear night, we may be surprised to awaken in the morning and learn that a heavy snow has fallen.

This change from season to season is *ku*; the season and the changes clearly exist, but they do not rely on conscious action. We do not contribute to the changes of season with our consciousness, nor are the seasons themselves "aware" of their own changes. The process of change from one season to another has no *shiki*, no visible form, but this process still clearly exists.

In karate-do, the meaning of *kara (ku)* is the same. For example, when students first learn a *kata*, they must concentrate on the movements, involving themselves completely in conscious attention to every detail. A great deal of conscious thought is required, and complete attention must be given to *shiki*, the physical form of the *kata*. After many repetitions, however, the student does not consciously think so much about the physical nature of the movements; they become more natural, and the body remembers the sequence. The form (*shiki*) is becoming emptiness (*ku*). *Shiki soku ze ku.*

After thousands of repetitions, the *kata* becomes part of the nature of the student. When we watch experts perform their *kata*, we sometimes feel that they are moving in another plane of existence. They are no longer doing the *kata*; the *kata* is "doing itself" on their body. No conscious thought is given to

89

the physical form of the *kata*. This complete emptiness (*ku*) is the same emptiness in the change of seasons. No conscious thought is involved, and the *shiki* (the different seasons or the techniques of the *kata*) is expressed through his emptiness. *Ku soku ze shiki.*

In the *kata* Kanku Dai, the first movements are visual representations of *shiki soku ze ku, ku soku ze shiki*. The hands move together and raise above the head toward the sky, then

break apart, moving in a wide arc to come together again in front of the center of the body. Together they are form; apart they are emptiness. Then they come back together. Form becomes emptiness; emptiness becomes form.

In the Zen tradition, pupils are taught that *shiki soku ze ku, ku soku ze shiki* means that positive becomes negative, hot becomes cold, gain becomes loss, and so on. The phrase is an exposition on the belief that the universe is dynamically balanced and in a constant state of flow between its polarities.

In karate-do, the expression of form through emptiness can only be found in the process of repeated performance of the techniques. Some modern instructors might be heard to say, "practice this technique until it becomes 'second nature.'" But in its ultimate manifestation, the technique that has been practiced thousands of times is not a "second nature" technique at all. It is, in fact, an outward representation (*shiki*) of the manifestation of the emptiness (*ku*) of the performer. *Ku soku ze shiki.*

The benefit of this state of mind in free-sparring or in a real fight is that the mind does not have to think about the situation nor devise a strategy for one kind of opponent or another. Indeed, in a time of crisis, students who have trained rigorously to achieve this state will simply "release their mind," throwing out all conscious thoughts, allowing the techniques they have practiced so often to be performed through their bodies. No matter what the opponent does, the response of the student will be proper and strong, and it will often appear that the response comes before the attack.

We have all heard about the masters who seem to know what their opponent is going to do before he does it, and *shiki soku ze ku, ku soku ze shiki* is the reason. We can no more successfully attack such a person than we can stop the snow from falling by punching at the sky.

It is impossible to attack emptiness.

HARAGEI—SPEAKING FROM THE GUT

Several years ago, one of my younger students accompanied me to a national conference of karate leaders. I told the student that paying close attention to the proceedings would help him understand the inner workings of a large karate organization as well as its Japanese and American leaders.

My student took my advice seriously and hung on every word in the day-long meeting.

Near the end of the meeting, a detailed discussion was held about a delicate public relations matter. My teacher, who was chairman of the meeting, spoke heatedly in Japanese with some of the other instructors, while the rest of us also offered our comments. Finally, someone proposed that the chairman be allowed to handle the difficult matter and that I draft a letter to the individuals involved. There were no objections to this proposal, but I noted my teacher was silent during the discussion and voting.

When the voting was over, I looked directly at my instructor and said, "Sensei, is this the way you want this matter handled?"

"Yes," he replied, looking directly into my eyes for several seconds. Once or twice, his eyes blinked rapidly.

"*Hai!*" I said, indicating that I understood.

When my student and I got back to my hotel room, we went over our notes from the meeting.

"When are you going to draft this letter and statement for Sensei? Do you want to do it now, or wait until we get back home?" my student asked.

"I'm not going to draft it at all," I replied. "Sensei said he doesn't want it done that way. I'll have to wait until I can talk to him alone to find out how he wants it done."

"But I distinctly heard him say yes when you asked him about it," the student protested.

"He said yes," I explained, "but he clearly meant no. I saw it in the way he blinked."

Reflecting on the incident, I'm sure my student thought I was crazy or had been to one too many meetings. But I was not confused. I was correct. When I talked to my teacher later, he expalined the different approach he wanted to take on the matter.

What my teacher had said to me with his mouth was contradictory to what he said to me with his belly. The Japanese call

this *haragei* (stomach art or belly talk). The Japanese people can say one thing but mean something entirely different. *Haragei* is the method of communicating by gut feeling, facial expression, length and timing of silence, and interpretation of seemingly meaningless sounds like "ah, ah, ah" and "eh-h-h-h . . ."

Haragei grew partly out of the well-known Japanese distrust of straightforward communication, and partly out of the racial, cultural, and social homogeneity of their society. After being raised with the same values for the past thousand years, they can be reasonably sure of their neighbor's reaction to any given situation.

By virtue of our great cultural diversity, Americans are taught to be specific. *Haragei* can be a source of great frustration to Americans dealing with Japanese karate instructors, but the problem is by no means limited to karate.

In his excellent book, *The Japanese Mind*, Robert Christopher tells the story of an American journalist who collided with *haragei* while interviewing an elder statesman of Japan's ruling Liberal Democratic Party. He asked the old man how many months it would be before the Prime Minister would be forced to resign. The statesman wanted the journalist to have the correct information, but he did not want to be quoted. So he turned to *haragei*.

Repeatedly muttering, *"Muzakashii ne,"* ("difficult question"), the statesman used his finger to trace the number seven on his desk top.

The American journalist, a long-time resident of Japan, got the message. But such has not always been the case for many American karate people who have met their Japanese counterparts in political settings. The communications gap has contributed greatly to a continuing rift between karate leaders from both countries.

The problem, however, could be alleviated if American karate leaders learn to look to their Japanese counterparts not just for the answer, but for the *haragei* behind the answer.

CHAMPION BY COINCIDENCE

When I was a teenage brown belt, there was very little I wanted more than to be a karate tournament champion. Tournaments were the "in thing" among my peers in those days, and all my heroes were big-name champions.

One of my main seniors, in fact, was a legend in Midwest karate competition. After going undefeated for three years, his name on an entry form made him an instant tournament favorite.

No matter that he was six-feet, four-inches tall and I was a skinny five-feet, six-inches. I still wanted to be like him.

My teacher, however, told me to forget it. He said there was no way to train for a tournament, that true karate-do is an art attained one day at a time. He told me to bury my useless notions on training for tournaments and just do my best every day in class. If I trained hard, he said, I would develop a punch and kick too strong to be blocked, and a block too strong to be penetrated.

Besides, he noted, concentrating too much on winning tournaments would detract from what I was trying to accomplish in daily practice.

"Goal very bad," he said. "Only train every day. Pretty soon, karate very strong and tournament no problem. Empty mind, and you will be surprised. Don't think, 'I must be champion.' Too much ego this way. Don't think. Just do. Then, someday you be practicing in tournament and you win. Better to be champion by coincidence."

My youthful exuberance told me not to buy any of that Japanese philosophical stuff, so I went to my seniors and asked them how to train to be a champion.

"Be sure to do wind sprints every day," one of them advised. "And don't forget push-ups and sit-ups and squats. Conditioning is the key to winning."

"Practice mental imaging," another advised. "Every day for a month before a tournament, I play a movie in my head of all my potential opponents, and I see myself being beaten by them, and then I analyze how they did it, and I replay the movie with me winning."

It seemed every champion I talked to had a different formula for success, and since there was a tournament almost every week in the Midwest, I had a chance to try all their prescriptions.

None of their plans worked.

What I got was torn muscles, black eyes, split lips, and lots of tournament losses. I gave up after about a year of this torture. I decided I neither liked tournaments nor had what it took to win one. It was relatively easy to put tournaments out of my mind for a year.

Then, I found myself in an unusual situation. As was my custom, I embarked on my weekly 250-mile trip to train with a Japan Karate Association instructor in the Midwest. Normally, I would leave home Friday around 6:00 p.m. and arrive five hours later. This gave me a chance to practice in the *dojo* for a couple of hours and then sleep on the floor until Saturday morning training. This time, however, my faithful car had other ideas.

First, there was a flat tire, then a broken radiator hose, and finally a terrible thunderstorm. By the time I arrived, it was almost 4:00 a.m., and the place was empty. There was no way I was going to call the instructor at that hour, so I parked on a dark side street and tried to sleep.

I awoke with a terrific cramp in my left thigh. Somehow, I had managed to twist myself into a pretzel shape in the front seat of my car, around the floor-mounted gearshift, and awoke feeling like I had been in a fight—a fight I lost. Much to my dismay, I found the cramp in my leg would not go away, no matter what I did.

When the teacher arrived at the dojo at 9:00, he commented on how terrible I looked. When I explained what had happened, he told me to take a shower and make myself presentable.

He was hosting an inter-dojo tournament, and he didn't want guests from other organizations thinking his students were dirty and unkempt.

An hour later, I was sitting at my usual place at the time-keeper's table, desperately trying to stay awake. In fact, the only thing keeping me awake was the extreme pain in my leg.

Suddenly, my teacher walked up to the table and said, "We have four teams competing, but our team is one man short. You fight today."

"Oh, Sensei!" I whimpered. "I can't fight today. I'm sick, and my leg is shot. I can't even walk, much less fight."

"You fight," he said firmly.

"Yes, Sensei!" I shouted. In that *dojo*, one did not argue with the teacher.

To make matters worse, the individual brackets were not working out evenly, and my teacher told me I would also compete in the individual competition.

So, against my will and decidedly against the wishes of my body, I competed.

To this day, I have no recollection of what happened during that tournament. I was so tired, I moved as if I was sleepwalking. They tell me I faced seven opponents that afternoon, and that I performed the *kata* Kanku Sho, but I really don't remember much—just an aching body and a leg that felt like it was on fire.

They also tell me that I won my team match and all my individual matches, and that I took first place in *kumite* (sparring) and second place in *kata*. And since I do have two trophies, I suppose they are telling me the truth.

All I know for sure is that today I tell my students, "Don't set fleeting goals. Just train every day and make your karate strong. Just empty your mind and practice every day. Someday, whether you are attacked on the street or competing in a tournament, you will be surprised at the results.

"Better to be a champion by coincidence."

ONE THE HARD WAY

One of my senior students recently had a strong talk with me. He said someone had to sit down and explain to me that I was not protecting my health or social life.

"You just spend too many hours working," he said, "and I don't think anyone appreciates your efforts as much as they should, and, well, why don't you just take a break? Just take a vacation. We can handle the classes in the *dojo*, and you could just sneak away for a while and rest. Besides, all the extra work you do doesn't really pay. You make it too hard on yourself."

I sincerely appreciated the student's concern, and I was touched by his interest. He was wrong, of course; I could do lots more than I currently do, if I would just stick to it. But he was sincere, and his thoughtfulness instantly brought to mind the words of a former teacher: "Hard way is best way."

I was always taught the "hard way" was the only way to learn karate. In the Buddhist tradition, the Japanese are taught that there are two ways to go through life. One is the way of *jiriki* (the way of self-denial and self-reliance) and the other is *tariki* (the way of reliance on others). My teacher explained *jiriki* as the way of walking along the road, facing and overcoming all obstacles. *Tariki*, he said, is like riding through life in a limousine with a chauffeur at the wheel. He said most people go through life in the *tariki* manner, and they never gain real strength or deep insight into themselves.

When he spoke of *jiriki* as a way in karate, he called it *nangyo-do* (the way of hardship).

"If you take the easy way," he warned, "you cannot learn karate-do."

I think most people in karate think they are taking the hard way, but I also think they miss the main point of *jiriki*. The way of self-denial and self-reliance is not just going through hard training in the *dojo*. Even if students are able to do 1,000 push-ups and practice for hours, it does not mean they are taking the hard way in the sense of *jiriki* or *nangyo*. These terms encompass life itself—both in and out of the *dojo*.

When I try to explain *jiriki* and *tariki* to my own students, I frequently use the example of one of my seniors, Leslie Safar.

Safar is the most senior student of Japan Karate Association eighth degree black belt Teruyuki Okazaki, and today ranks in the fifth *dan* (black belt degree). He has a very successful *dojo* called the South Jersey Karate Club. By karate standards, Safar is a very successful man. But the manner in which he attained his success is clearly the way of *jiriki* and *nangyo*— self-reliance and hardship.

Safar was born in Hungary, but was forced to escape from his homeland during the 1956 Communist uprising. When he arrived on the East Coast, he could neither speak English nor find any of the fabled streets paved with gold. To help relieve some of the tension, he would lift weights in a Philadelphia gym. Someone at the gym brought in a book on karate, and Safar was mesmerized. The problem, of course, was that there weren't any karate instructors in the Philadelphia area in the late 1950s.

101

Finally, one of his gymmates heard that a Mr. Sugiura was attending college in Philadelphia and that he was a karate expert. Toshio Sugiura was a second-degree black belt from Keio University, the first collegiate karate club founded by Gichin Funakoshi (karate's founder) in Japan.

"We just sent Mr. Sugiura a message," Safar recalls, "saying that if he would teach karate, we would be his students, and we kept bugging him until he agreed."

After two years of training under Sugiura in a ramshackle building with too little heat and too many splinters in the floor, Safar was introduced to Japan Karate Association master, Teruyuki Okazaki.

"Neither Mr. Okazaki nor I could speak English," Safar says, "so we got along pretty well. The only problem was that we could only communicate physically. We would just stand and punch or kick or block for hours. Sometimes we would get so tired we couldn't walk, but I kept at it, and we spent a lot of time together outside the *dojo*."

Indeed, the only real communication Okazaki kept pounding into Safar was that he could not give up. The hard way was the only way Okazaki knew, and it was the way he passed along to Safar.

"There were only six of us who started training with Mr. Okazaki," Safar says, "and I'm the only one who continued. The thing about the hard training was that I was struggling to learn English, trying to figure out how to make a living, and no matter how bad things got, I could always fall back on my training for strength. I am a firm believer that the hard way of training is the only way to teach a person to reach inside himself and find out what he is really made of.

"When I was training in the early days," Safar adds, "I quit lots of times, and every time I did, I found out that I didn't quite have enough strength to face all the problems in everyday life. I think it made me say to myself, 'Sure, life is tough, and this problem or that problem is really bad, but it isn't nearly as tough as trying to survive a workout at the *dojo*.' I figured that if I could survive the training, I could survive anything."

Today, Safar's good friend, Ray Dalke, says, "If you want to see what the hard way is all about, you have to look at Les Safar. Here he was in a strange land, couldn't even speak the language, and he went in day after day and put himself through torture."

And what does Dalke think of Safar's abilities? "If I'm ever in a bad situation, physically or otherwise, I want Les Safar on my side," Dalke says. "I honestly believe that if someone wanted to fight with him, they would have to kill him to discourage him. Just knocking him out or seriously injuring him wouldn't help. He is so determined, there is no doubt he would keep coming back again and again."

Today, as he moves about his modern, computerized *dojo*, Safar is at ease with himself and his surroundings. He is a man whose joy with life is not concealed. He has many plans for the future, and his admirers say he approaches it with single-minded determination. His detractors might call it "unmovable stubbornness."

No matter what you call it, there is no waver in his voice when you tell him things are tough and you don't know how you're going to get through.

"Listen," he says firmly, "if you train the hard way, you can do anything."

Somehow, I think he's right.

BUDO NO KOKORO
(THE SPIRIT OF *BUDO*)

Reinhold Messner and Peter Habler were the first men to climb Mt. Everest without carrying a supply of oxygen. Sometime later, Messner became the first man to climb Everest alone without a supply of oxygen. Incredibly, even though Messner is no longer a young man, he is still scaling the heights.

I was mentioning this to a friend some time ago, and he remarked, "The guy is nuts. He's going to take the big swan dive into eternity one of these days."

"Of course he is," I said. "He knows that, and he wouldn't have it any other way. But he's certainly not crazy."

"Right," my friend countered sarcastically, "and I'm supposed to take your answer as gospel—you, who still thinks that by following the instructor blindly you can miraculously become Japanese. Baloney!"

But my friend was wrong. For the last 10 years, I have clearly understood that, even though I follow the teachings of my Japanese instructors blindly in the *dojo*, I will never be Japanese. Indeed, no matter how hard I might try, I will never be admitted to the hallowed halls of "samuraihood."

This became painfully clear to me a decade ago when I was training in a class under a famous Japanese karate instructor. I was doing something wrong and the instructor patiently explained the correct way to proceed. He took great pains to help me understand, and I appreciated it. However, I was a black belt, and the person in line next to me was a green belt. After carefully explaining what I needed to do to correct the flaws in my technique, the instructor turned to the green belt next to me, who happened to be a Japanese-American, and said scornfully, "You should know better; you are Japanese!"

I am still offended by that remark today.

What upsets so many traditionalists today is, try as they might, they never seem to gain acceptance from their Japanese instructors. There always seems to be a gulf between sincere, American students and their Japanese instructors. Unfortunately, this rift has led to the loss of many Americans who, if accorded simple respect, would have stayed in karate training and helped the art grow.

American traditionalists should suppress their emotions and take a step back. They should try to see things as they actually are, accept them, and proceed in their training.

"Oh, fine," you say. "And exactly how are things?"

I think I have an answer, and it is best illustrated in Bill Hosokawa's column in *The Pacific Citizen*. Hosokawa calls his

column "From the Frying Pan," and on November 30, 1984, he led it with the catchy title of "Panic in the Sumo Ring."

According to Hosokawa, a young Samoan named Salevaa Fuauli, a 20-year-old carrying about 470 pounds on his freakish frame, entered the autumn Grand Sumo Tournament in Tokyo under his sumo name of Konishiki.

Konishiki's sin was not so much that he invaded a sacrosanct Japanese sport, nor that he entered the tournament without going through the arduous *sumotori* apprenticeship that is supposed to produce men of superior quality and attitude. Indeed, Konishiki's mortal sin was that, without any officially sanctioned training as a sumo wrestler, he managed to score perfect victories over all but one of his many famous opponents, losing only in the grand championship match and finishing second in the prestigious tournament.

Probably even worse than placing second, Konishiki boldly and innocently informed the Japanese press that, unlike his foreign counterpart, Hawaiian Takamiyama, who took out Japanese citizenship, he has no intention of taking sumo seriously. With childish innocence, Konishiki said sumo was something he thought he could do well to make money and have fun, and his greatest goal in life was to return to Hawaii with his prize money and open a supermarket.

According to Hosokawa, the Japanese reaction to Konishiki was less than friendly. Indeed, Hosokawa relates verified accounts of high-level *sumotori* suggestions that Konishiki be deliberately and severely injured during practice sessions. Some famous sumo wrestlers are quoted as saying Konishiki's *chanko-nabe*, a high-calorie staple stew dish for sumo wrestlers, should be laced with sugar to make him susceptible to diabetes.

Otherwise respectable businessmen, it seems, suggested without subtlety that Konishiki be given an "injection." In Japanese parlance, this means he should be bribed to throw his matches for sums ranging from 250,000 to 1 million yen (approximately $1,000–$4,000), depending on the importance of the particular match.

The celebrated Japanese xenophobia apparently is alive and well and living in Tokyo.

This is not to say, of course, that the Japanese karate instructors who have come to the United States and lived as Americans would even consider the drastic, unethical and immoral actions of their Tokyo counterparts.

What this should say to all dedicated, sincere students of traditional Japanese karate is that you should see things exactly as they are, without embellishment. You are not Japanese, and your teachers know it.

If you are practicing karate and clinging to your Japanese instructors with visions of samuraihood dancing in your mind, you should re-think your position.

There is only one reason to give yourself over to a lifetime commitment of hard training: Take pride in dedicating your life to a task that will give you unbounded joy and deep, personal satisfaction at the mere thought of pursuing it.

Any other reason will not be adequate.

IS KARATE AN ART OR A SPORT?

At a recent instructors' conference of the American JKA Karate Associations (AJKA), two questions spurred much debate: "Is karate an art or a sport, and how should it be taught and presented to the students?"

Since those in the room were so-called "traditionalists," there was immediate consensus that karate-do is, first and foremost, an art. However, modern karate certainly has a sporting aspect, and that's where the debate got heated. Just how can an instructor teach an art and simultaneously present it as a sport?

The problem is karate-do originally was an art of self-defense. Following its reorganization during the Meiji era (1868-1912), the art was transformed into a *do* (path) form; the techniques that were once used for self-protection became the focal point of an art of self-perfection.

Nevertheless, until the mid-1950s, karate in Japan retained its foundation of *ikken-hisatsu* (killing an opponent with one blow). The teaching methods were based on the concept that human beings could look deeply into themselves and develop better character if they trained with the idea of a life-and-death struggle foremost in their minds. This would encourage them to take their art seriously, and would also prepare them for any self-defense situation that might arise.

With the advent of sport karate, however, the techniques began to change a bit. Obviously, students could not be allowed to make actual contact with their potentially lethal blows, so contact had to be controlled. At the same time, if everybody tried to deliver a decisive "killing" blow, the competition would be somewhat slow. This would mean few spectators would come to see the matches. Outside of Japan, in particular, the potential audiences could not be expected to be educated in the precepts of *budo*. They would, therefore, by and large find boring tournaments recognizing only firmly rooted, killing blows.

The solution to this dilemma emerged slowly over about 25 years, and it entailed finding ways to make karate competition more exciting for the spectators while retaining its essence as a way of self-denial and human perfection. Fighting stances gradually became a little higher, and the contestants got up on their toes and bounced around a little more. Then *kata* started to get fancy. In *kata*, a technique that in the old days was recognized for its effectiveness and intensity, was now more recognized for its flashy execution.

In most schools around the world this is no problem. Instructors who want to teach the old way do so and ignore tournaments; instructors who want their students to compete, teach sport and how to "catch the point."

But for us old boys, who were trained in the rather austere fashion of 25 years ago, it is a problem—a big problem. We know our roots lie in karate-do as an art, and we cling to the idea of *ikken-hisatsu* as the best way of looking inside oneself and finding out of what one is truly made. At the same time, we recognize that sport karate is not going to go away, and we know it can be a key tool in promoting understanding and acceptance among people and even nations.

So, what is our solution? We couldn't unanimously agree on one. Some feel the old ways should be followed exactly, and some feel more emphasis should be given to sport training.

My feeling is that a big change should occur in the *dojo* where traditional karate-do is taught seriously. I don't think there should be any change in the fundamental precepts of karate-do as a way of life, nor in the fundamental, rigorous training methods designed to lead the student to awareness, emotional control, and humility. But it does seem to me a new course in traditional karate ought to be offered. The way we

might solve the problem is to teach as we always have, emphasizing the deeper meanings of karate training, and then at some point—levels below black belt—start teaching sport karate as a separate entity.

This idea runs contrary to the feelings of most of my teachers, but I really think it might work. There can be no doubt, for example, that the long hours spent in long, low stances in most traditional *dojo*, and the traditional painstaking attention to details of body and stance dynamics would benefit any student in competition. Hard conditioning is important to development in almost any sport.

By first developing the basics, the student would then find it much easier to get up on his toes and dance around in competitive fashion, supported by a thoroughly strengthened mind and body. Catching a point is far easier than killing an opponent with one perfectly executed blow and, generally speaking, can be learned faster.

This is a difficult time for traditional karate-do, and it creates hard times for traditional karate instructors.

Nevertheless, if traditional karate-do is going to retain its essence as a martial art and simultaneously enjoy the popularity that international sport engenders, the time is now for instructors to consider their options.

WHAT'S A NICE GIRL LIKE YOU DOING HERE?

A few years ago, a high-ranking Japanese instructor was visiting my *dojo* for a black belt rank examination. A lot of people were taking the test that day, and quite a few of them were women.

Part of the rank examination for second-degree black belt involves sparring against several opponents, and one of the examinees for the second degree happened to be a woman. When we got to the sparring segment, the instructor told me to pair the examination cards, which I did without much thought. When the names were called, however, the woman (who was of average size) was paired with a very tall, powerfully built man.

"Oh, no!" the instructor whispered to me. "You can't put a girl out there with a big guy like that. Find a girl she can fight with."

"But, Sensei," I protested, "she is the only woman testing at this level. The only other women here are brown belts."

"Then put her with a brown belt," he said firmly. "We can't let a pretty little girl like her get beat up by some big guy like that."

In all my years in karate, I have always tried very hard to show respect for my teachers and seniors, and I honestly find it incomprehensible that a sincere student would refuse the direct instructions of his teacher. But at that moment, I stepped out of character like I never had before.

"No, Sensei," I said firmly. "I will not do that. She is my student, and she has worked just as hard as the men have to achieve her present level. To single her out now because she is a female would be insulting and degrading. If she wants to rank in the second degree black belt, she will have to do it just like everyone else. If she can't handle this guy, she doesn't deserve the rank. I won't do it."

After a few seconds of intense staring, the instructor said to me, "OK, OK! But if she gets hurt, you take the responsibility!"

"Good!" I said sharply.

I find that conversation upsetting even today. For a long time, I would argue with myself that the instructor, being Japanese, was a victim of his culture. He was just acting the way he has always been taught to act, I reasoned.

But I really think it goes deeper than that, and I think it is one of the fundamental problems with karate and other martial

arts in America today. It is not so much that Japanese culture, externally at least, holds women in lower regard than men, although that is certainly part of it. It is more, to my way of thinking, that karate was introduced to this country as a macho activity for men only. While younger students may not remember it, I certainly recall the days of "fear-no-man" advertising. The advertising slant was centered around the 98-pound weakling who, by taking the appropriate course in body building or self-defense, could chase the bullies away and have an adoring female on his arm. Karate itself, when demonstrated by qualified people, leaned heavily toward board and brick breaking and similar feats of strength.

Traditional karate today seems to have veered away from the fear-no-man syndrome, but I am still amazed at the number of demonstrations that involve feats of strength. In some ways, the syndrome is even healthier and more bizarre than it was in the 1960s. Today, people have trucks run over them, and one poor fellow even lost his life trying to smash some ice with his forehead.

If karate is an art (and I believe it is) designed to teach people self-defense, provide them with good physical health, and help them develop into confident, graceful human beings, the macho attitude must be put to rest.

In my *dojo*, and in every *dojo* I visit around the country, the number of women students is growing steadily. Of course, the reasons women have for pursuing karate are as varied as the men's reasons. That is not the point. The point is that karate—indeed, all *budo*—should be for everyone, young or old, male or female. In the modern world, there simply is no place for the old attitudes about women in combative arts and sports.

When I talk to the instructors I am charged with developing, I always tell them the same thing: "Don't teach 'men's karate' or 'children's karate' or 'women's karate.' Just teach karate, and let everybody train. Don't tell the women they don't have to do knuckle push-ups to protect their soft, pretty hands, or that they don't have to do push-ups at all because they aren't strong enough. Just teach karate, and don't worry about it."

If one is running a health spa or social group, I suppose it would be a good idea to treat everybody differently to keep them happy so they will keep paying their dues. If one is running a karate *dojo*, however, one should be engaged in one business and one business only: teaching karate.

If I had allowed the instructor to treat my female student differently that day several years ago, I know for certain that she would never have come back to the *dojo*. As it is, however, she is now an experienced second degree black belt in the American JKA Karate Associations.

By the way, during her examination, that "pretty little girl" jumped at the big guy she was facing and repeatedly drove him backward with flurries of skillful, powerful punches and kicks. As I watched her, I couldn't control my wide smile.

"Just teach karate," I thought, "and everything else will take care of itself."

HOW TO PUT EVERYDAY LIVING INTO KARATE

Gichin Funakoshi, the man who introduced karate-do to Japan, left his followers with 20 precepts that contain the essence of the art as a way of life. One of the most famous of these maxims is, *"Arai-yuru mono wo karate-ka seyo, soko ni myo-mi ari."* Or, "put your everyday living into karate and you will find *myo.*"

Myo has no English equivalent. Broadly speaking, however, it refers to a natural, exquisite, unencumbered state of mind. In fact, *myo* is the most natural state of mind in which a person responds to an event. This response is automatic, and the person is in perfect harmony with the environment. When you experience *myo*, your state of mind is much like that of the bee building its hive, or the spider spinning its web—natural and flowing.

How do you put your everyday living into karate? As a starting point, exercise your mind to make it more aware of your surroundings.

Consider this example: What should you do if you get into your car and someone hiding in the back seat attacks you? The correct answer is, if someone is lurking in the back seat of your car, don't get in the car. There is little anyone can do when caught in certain situations. In the preceding attack, there are certain techniques you could use, but their success requires acute awareness of lapses in the attacker's attention. If you have such awareness, you should sense danger before entering the car.

People who master karate-do can defend themselves in any situation. This isn't because they have perfect fighting ability. Rather, such people are highly aware of themselves and their environment. Avoidance is the best self-defense, but to avoid danger, you must be aware that danger exists. This is where putting your everyday living into karate comes into play.

Awareness can't be obtained; it must be realized. Your ultimate goal is to maintain concentration in the *tanden* (lower abdomen) 24 hours a day. While using the *tanden* as a focal point, you can develop awareness of the environment.

Recall the example of the mugger in the back seat of your car. Consider the value of training your mind to focus on the *tanden* every time you approach a car door. When you are ready to fall asleep at night, visualize your car, then picture yourself

approaching it. Lower your breathing to the *tanden*, and look in the back seat. Imagine an empty back seat and see yourself calmly and securely get into your car. Visualize an attacker in the back seat, and imagine calmly walking away to call the police.

When you actually walk to your car, do the same thing, and you will eventually overcome the fear of attack.

To take another example, assume you just entered a room full of people, most of whom you do not know. A friend calls to you from the other side of the room and asks you to come over. Without thinking, you walk through the crowd to your friend.

If you do this, however, you are missing an opportunity to put your everyday living into karate.

Rather than mindlessly walking through the crowd, pause for a few seconds. Lower your breathing to your *tanden* and see how many people are in the room. Find the exits and look at the windows to see if they can be used as exits. Now determine whether the people are in small groups or scattered. Finally, consider the atmosphere: is it tense or relaxed? If there are a lot of people between you and your friend, maybe you should walk around the group rather than through it.

If you sit down, think about your chair in terms of self-defense. For instance, is it a soft chair, one that prevents you from rising quickly? Does it have arms that restrict you? Will the chair's legs slide on the floor, or will they stick? Is it possible to sit with your back to the wall for protection? These are all important questions you must consider.

Also, think about how you sit. If you bend over, grasp the chair with both hands and pull it to you, you are open to attack. Sit straight and maintain feeling in the *tanden*. Sit and rise from the center of your body.

Such thinking may seem like a game, but it will protect you from danger. As you put your everyday living into karate, you conquer fear because you train your mind to be aware of yourself and your environment.

Exercise your mind this way and you will understand that self-defense includes looking both ways before crossing a street. Through experience and training, you learn to detect the danger of crossing a street without looking. Similarly, you also learn by experience to handle sharp knives carefully.

Visualization exercises heighten your sense of sight, hearing, and feeling. By putting your everyday living into karate in this fashion, you make yourself less vulnerable to attack.

This is the first step toward *myo*.

WINNING AND LOSING

The Zen instructor, Kaishu (1808-1878), was crossing a river in a boat one day with several pupils. It was raining violently, and the waves were tossing the boat to and fro. As the storm worsened, several of the young Buddhists became so frightened that they cried and shouted prayers to Avalokitesvara, the Buddhist goddess of love. All the while, Kaishu sat calmly in meditation, breathing evenly and smiling faintly.

When the boat reached the shore, one of his pupils blurted, "Sensei, weren't you scared?"

Kaishu giggled and then explained, "A man is worthless if he can't take care of himself and let his *do* (way) sustain him in bad times. The goddess must be laughing herself silly at all of you."

* * *

I use this story to teach my students the importance of training hard and maintaining dedication to the way of life (*do*) of the art of karate. Karate-do is a path, I tell them, which will provide strength in times of crisis—not only in the *dojo*, but in everyday life as well.

Several years ago, I faced the most difficult business crisis I have ever encountered, and the story about Kaishu took on new meaning for me. I was faced with a situation that could have resulted in a hostile takeover of a large portion of a business I was involved in. Since I am as conscientious as anyone in my desire to earn a living and support my family, I gave the matter a lot of deep thought and consideration.

I tried every kind of maneuvering I could think of to avoid the problem and put the matter to rest, but the harder I tried, the worse it got. After many sleepless nights, it became apparent to me that I could not win. The other side was going to control me, and there was nothing I could do about it.

A good friend, who was sympathetic to my cause, told me to tense my body and resolve myself to the loss. "Cut your losses and go on from there," he said. "Your enemies have you on the run, and you might as well resolve yourself to it." I agreed, and immediately began feeling sorry for myself.

That same night, I was teaching an advanced class of black belts. One of them was having a terrible time defending himself against the overpowering onslaught of one of his seniors in free sparring. He was being chased around the *dojo* like a frightened rabbit, repeatedly being swept to the floor, punched, and kicked.

"No, don't run!" I shouted. "Be strong! You have to stand up to your opponent and become more skillful, no matter how much it hurts!"

"But, Sensei," he pleaded, "I can't beat this guy. He's killing me!"

121

"No, no, no!" I shouted. "Remember what Master Funakoshi said. One of his famous twenty precepts is, 'Do not think you have to win. Rather, think that you do not have to lose.' Do you understand?"

"Yes," the student wearily replied. "I understand."

In the same instant, I realized that the student really did not understand. And I realized that I did not understand, either.

Do not think you have to win. Rather, think that you do not have to lose, I said to myself. The approach I took with my business was wrong all along.

After all these years, I haven't learned anything, I thought. Here I was, scared about an outcome I couldn't control, and I completely disregarded a fundamental precept of my art. I concentrated fully on winning my business confrontation, but I lost sight of the best strategy. I was trying to remain calm like Kaishu on the boat, but I was missing the point.

The next day, I called my "enemies" and calmly told them it was time for a meeting. I would come to them and discuss everything, I said. I promised to be reasonable. They agreed, and I slept peacefully that night with Funakoshi's precept playing over and over again in my mind: You don't have to win, but you don't have to lose.

I sat calmly at the meeting the next day, listening to the complaints and demands, much like Kaishu contemplated the storm. Not once did I react in an emotional way, and I did not defend myself against the bitter accusations.

When the shouting died down, I simply said, "That is all well and good, gentlemen. I understand your position perfectly, and I even agree that you are right about a lot of things. However, you must clearly understand that all of this has no meaning for me. I am not interested in your proposals, and I have no regard for your plans. Take what you want from me and go on. I have survived for many years without giving in to demands like yours, and I will survive many more years in the same way. You can take whatever you want, and with my blessing. The one thing you cannot do is defeat me in this. You cannot defeat me because there is no longer anything to fight about. Not only can you have the portions of this business you desire, but you can have all of it. I resign. No hard feelings, I hope."

"Wait a minute," they protested. "We just want these changes made. We don't want you to resign. That would kill the business completely. Besides, we have a legal right to make these changes."

"You certainly do," I answered, "and I have a legal right to resign. Take the whole business with my blessing."

While this may sound like an age-old bluff or childish petulance ("If you don't play my way, I'll take my toys and go home"), it was different. Much to my surprise, the attitude of my enemies changed instantly. Suddenly, they were cooperative and conciliatory. We were able to reach reasonable compromises, and the business was saved.

Looking back on it now, I realize that neither side "won" the battle in the classical sense. We just mutually resolved to go on and try to work with each other.

Since that time several years ago, I have always tried to keep Funakoshi's precept firmly in my mind in times of business crisis: Do not think that you have to win. Rather, think that you do not have to lose. It really works.

KARATE AS A LIFETIME ART

Throughout my life, one of the hardest things I have tried to understand is the Eastern view of the world—the value of intuition over postulation—as opposed to the logical, rational view of the West.

I was taught that Westerners view nature as an entity apart from man—something to be conquered, subjugated, controlled and changed—while Easterners view man as an integral element of nature, an element that should exist in accord with natural laws. Western man fights against nature from the outside; Eastern man fights against himself to create a more pleasant existence from the inside.

Years ago, while struggling with this new idea, I explained my confusion to a famous karate master. He told me that what you see, or how you view the world, is what you believe, and he told me a story to illustrate his point.

He said that a young prince lived with his father in a palace on the shores of the ocean. The prince led an idyllic life and daily strolled along his private beach to gaze out over the water and watch the birds fly gently in the breeze. One day he was startled to suddenly see a large island appear with dragons and monsters cavorting and fighting all over it. As he jumped back, he was again startled by a resounding voice behind him: "What's the matter?"

Turning, the frightened prince saw a fierce-looking man wearing a black evening coat with large sleeves.

"Who are you, and where did that island and those monsters come from?" the prince stammered.

"Why, I created them!" laughed the man.

"Then you must be God!" the prince cried.

"Of course I'm God!" came the fierce reply.

Terrified, the prince ran home and blurted the whole story to his father.

"This man you saw," said the father calmly, "was he wearing a black evening coat with large sleeves?"

"Yes," answered the prince, "but what does that have to do with anything?"

"The man you saw was not God," replied the father. "He was a magician. All magicians wear black evening coats with large sleeves. I am a magician, too. The man you saw is my friend. Now, for the first time, you notice that I also wear such an evening coat. I asked my friend to create an illusion and frighten you so you could become a man and see things as they really are. You have lived in illusion long enough. There is no island, there are no monsters, and you are not a prince. We are common people, and it is time for you to know that. I created illusions for your happiness as a child. Go and see for yourself."

After realizing the truth of his father's words, the boy returned home where his father was drinking tea with his friend.

"Father," said the boy, "you were right, but I cannot accept this. If I can't be a prince, I think I would rather be dead."

"Fine," replied the father, beckoning his son to kneel before him. "My friend will now kill you."

The boy thought it was a joke until he saw the blade of the friend's sword descending upon him.

"Wait!" he cried. "I understand!"

Whereupon the three men wordlessly had a cup of tea and went out to tend the fields.

I now understand the karate view, which is that we are all like the prince, living with various illusions we believe to be true. The purpose of karate-do is to help us see things as they really are and to broaden the scope and depth of our understanding.

One of the cornerstones of karate philosophy is the breaking of attachments. This is based on the premise that people naturally feel attached to things and only a greater force than the attachments will make them let go.

This is easily illustrated by assuming you have $100 in your pocket. Until some greater force comes to bear, you will keep the money. The greater force that makes you release it may be a robbery, a bill to pay, or simply your desire to have something that costs $100. In any case, you remain attached to the money, just as the prince  remained attached to his illusion, until a greater force (in the prince's case, his impending death) makes you let go of it.

We live by memory and experience, and like the prince facing death, we tend to fear and avoid things that are beyond our experience. Even with strong motivation, we naturally try to retain our attachments.

The purpose of karate-do is to teach us to live fearlessly—not by memory, but in the present—without attachments to anything but life itself. Without illusion or attachment, we can live life like the cherry blossom: brilliantly, fulfilling a purpose, and then suddenly letting go of life when the purpose is fulfilled. This is called *isagi-yoku*: to let go of life when the time is right, without fear, regret, or second thoughts.

Admittedly, this is not an easy course to follow, and that is why karate is a lifetime art. There are many ever-changing illusions and attachments, and constant discipline is required to overcome them.

STIFF MIND, STIFF BODY

Even though I was only 12 years old when I started karate training, I was very stiff. I never had the hip and leg flexibility so common in most 12-year-olds. In fact, I was constantly irritated by my inability to do front and side splits as easily as my classmates.

Even after I had attained black belt ranking years later, I was still stiff. One day, while practicing with a high-ranking Japanese instructor, I was told, "Relax! Relax! Just stretch completely."

"Sensei," I replied, "I've never been able to stretch completely. My body's too stiff."

"No," he said with a smile, "your mind is too stiff. Stiff mind, stiff body. Release mind; body will follow."

I found that particularly mystifying, and I didn't believe it for a second. He might think my mind is stiff, but I know my body is stiff, I thought.

About three years later, I trained again under this same instructor. During warm-up exercises, he stopped in front of me. "Ho!" he said with a laugh. "Still stiff mind! Too bad. Must release mind."

More than 10 years later, I was still mystified by his comments, and I took the problem to Masatoshi Nakayama, Chief Instructor of the Japan Karate Association. I knew that one of Gichin Funakoshi's famous twenty precepts was *"Kokoro wa hanatan koto wo yosu"* ("Always be ready to release your mind"), but it puzzled me, and I asked Nakayama what it meant.

"An important saying in karate-do," he replied, "is 'there is no posture (*kamae*) in karate.' This applies directly to the attitude necessary in training or actual fighting. It means the student must not stiffen the body and make it rigid. One should always be relaxed and alert. In Japan, we say that one should be flexible like bamboo, which bends and snaps back when the wind blows. One who is stiff will break in the wind like a rigid oak tree.

"On the other hand, relaxation does not mean lack of alertness," Nakayama continued. "Sometimes I tell students there is posture, but no posture; that there is mental posture, but no physical posture. At the very highest levels of development, though, the karateka should have no posture at all—no posture of mind and no posture of body.

"This is very difficult to grasp, but it is essential in order to master karate-do," Nakayama added. "This concept was summarized in the 17th century by the Zen priest, Takuan, in his famous letter to the swordsman, Yagyu Munenori. Takuan told Yagyu that if you place your mind on the movements of your opponent, it will be filled with your opponent's movements. Likewise, if your mind is fixed on your opponent's sword, on your own sword, on the cutting of your opponent, or on the fear of being cut yourself, it will be totally absorbed by whatever it is fixed on. And defeat will be inevitable. Takuan's solution to the problem was to suggest the mind be placed nowhere—that it be spread throughout the entire body, concentrating on nothing in particular. That way, he said, the mind will serve whatever part of the situation needs immediate attention. If the arms need to move, the mind will move them; if the legs need to move, the mind will move them, too. He is saying that if the mind is placed nowhere, it will be everywhere.

"This philosophy arises directly from Zen's desire to have no attachments to anything," Nakayama noted. "The '*kara*' of karate comes from Mahayana Buddhism, and is also pronounced *ku*, meaning 'void' or 'nothingness.' Its original meaning was 'to be lacking in' or 'to be wanting in,' and it calls for the individual to escape from the rules and differences between good and bad, reality and illusion. This, according to Mahayana Buddhism, strengthens the individual's ethics in that if one is attached to nothing, one will naturally choose good over evil.

"I know this is difficult," Nakayama added, "but the essence of it is to let the mind go and act naturally. When a person first sits behind the wheel of a car, for example, a lot of attention must be given to details: the accelerator, the brake, the steering wheel, and so on. After a while, however, we don't consciously think about these things. We just get in the car and drive, and when we need to stop, we naturally put our foot on the brake pedal.

"This is the same process we use in karate-do," Nakayama concluded. "When we begin training, we have no posture of mind, no technique. If we are attacked, we respond naturally, and flail away at our opponent. As we study posture and technique, we devise strategies, movements, and we learn to defend ourselves and counter-attack. But this takes away our natural spontaneity, and our minds are fixed on specific postures, techniques, and strategies. After many years of training, we return to our natural state—that of transcending techniques, postures, and strategies—and we again respond without thought. Of course, after many years of training, we are able to respond much more efficiently and effectively. It takes a lifetime to attain this spontaneous mind, which is simultaneously nowhere and everywhere."

I thanked Nakayama for all this insight, but I still did not see how it related to my stiff body, and every time I stretched before a workout, I thought about it carefully.

Not long ago, I was in the *dojo* alone, stretching my legs before some *kata* practice. As usual, I thought about Nakayama's statements and tried to figure out how they related to my stiffness.

"The heck with it," I thought. "I'll never figure it out. I'm just stuck with a stiff body."

Frustrated, I forgot the whole thing and started thinking about the *kata* I was going to practice. Still stretching, I closed my eyes and visualized the movements of the *kata* in my mind, trying to focus on the special feeling of the particular form.

After a few minutes, I opened my eyes and looked at myself in the *dojo* mirror. I was stunned. There I was in the mirror in an almost complete side split position, and I hadn't realized it. Most incredible of all, there was no pain!

Pulling my legs around and crossing them in front of me, I stared at myself in the mirror, completely amazed. Then I laughed out loud. "Stiff mind, stiff body." The words came back to me in a rush.

"You idiot," I muttered. "There are things about this art you're never going to figure out."

Photographs

Randall Hassell, 7, 8, 63, 73, 97, 98 -
   (Courtesy of Jose M. Fraguas)
James Field, 12 - (Courtesy of Jose M. Fraguas)
Y. Konishi, 15 - (Courtesy of Jose M. Fraguas)
Osamu Ozawa, 16 - (Courtesy of the Author)
Teruo Chinen, 23 - (Courtesy of Jose M. Fraguas)
Edmond Otis, 24, 47, 48, 64, 74, 85 -
   (Courtesy of Edmond Otis)
Masatoshi Nakayama & Randall Hassell, 26 -
   (Courtesy of the Author)
James Yabe, 34, 36, 51, 86, 125 - (Courtesy of Jose M. Fraguas)
Shojiro Koyama, 39, 40 -
   (Courtesy of Shojiro Koyama. Archives Jose M. Fraguas)
Hirokazu Kanazawa, 44, 118, 121 -
   (Courtesy of Jose M. Fraguas)
Jorge Romero, 53, 89 - (Courtesy of Jose M. Fraguas)
Les Safar, 55, 90, 101, 103 - (Courtesy of Jose M. Fraguas)
R. Hassell, J. Yabe, L. Safar & E. Otis, 59 -
   (Courtesy of Jose M. Fraguas)
H. Kanazawa & T. Mikami, 60 - (Courtesy of Jose M. Fraguas)
Tsuguo Sakumoto, 67, 70 - (Courtesy of Jose M. Fraguas)
Masatoshi Nakayama, 77, 78 -
   (Courtesy of M. Nakayama. Archives Jose M. Fraguas)
Keinosuke Enoeda, 94 -
   (Courtesy of K. Enoeda. Archives Jose M. Fraguas)
M. Gustavson & Steven Casper, 105, 107 -
   (Courtesy of Markus Boesch)
M. Gustavson, 113, 115 - (Courtesy of Markus Boesch)
Eihachi Ota, 117 (Courtesy of Jose M. Fraguas)
Choju Hentona, 127 - (Courtesy of Jose M. Fraguas)
Karate Dojo, Naha, Okinawa, 131 -
   (Courtesy of Jose M. Fraguas)